Y0-BCR-747

ELECTRONIC DIRECT MARKETING

G. Scott Osborne

ELECTRONIC DIRECT MARKETING

65647

A SPECTRUM BOOK

Prentice-Hall, Inc., Englewood Cliffs, New Jersey 07632

Library of Congress Cataloging in Publication Data

Osborne, G. Scott.
   Electronic direct marketing.

   "A Spectrum Book."
   Bibliography: p.
   Includes index.
     1. Direct marketing. 2. Electronic marketing.
I. Title.
HF5415.122.082 1984   658.8'4   83-19174
ISBN 0-13-250689-0
ISBN 0-13-250671-8 (pbk.)

This book is available at a special discount when ordered in
bulk quantities. Contact Prentice-Hall, Inc., General
Publishing Division, Special Sales, Englewood Cliffs, N.J. 07632.

10 9 8 7 6 5 4 3 2 1

ISBN 0-13-250689-0

ISBN 0-13-250671-8 {PBK.}

Editorial/production supervision by Elizabeth Torjussen
Cover design © 1984 by Jeannette Jacobs
Manufacturing buyer: Pat Mahoney

Prentice-Hall International, Inc., *London*
Prentice-Hall of Australia Pty. Limited, *Sydney*
Prentice-Hall Canada Inc., *Toronto*
Prentice-Hall of India Private Limited, *New Delhi*
Prentice-Hall of Japan, Inc., *Tokyo*
Prentice-Hall of Southeast Asia Pte. Ltd., *Singapore*
Whitehall Books Limited, *Wellington, New Zealand*
Editora Prentice-Hall do Brasil Ltda., *Rio de Janeiro*

To my parents, Frank and Mary Lou

CONTENTS

PREFACE

Electronic Direct Marketing (EDM) is increasingly becoming the way to do business. Not only is it the fastest-growing form of marketing today; it will also be the way most of us will do business in the future.

If you are looking for ways to increase or expand your business in the most cost effective and profitable way possible, a businessperson just starting out, or a member of the public wanting to learn more about how this explosive marketing phenomenon will affect your life, this book is for you.

It will show you how to take advantage of the extraordinary marketing opportunities to be found in the electronic media. You will learn how to use television, radio, the telephone, and the new electronic technologies to market virtually any product or service more efficiently and profitably. You will be able to determine the feasibility of the application of EDM to your product, business, or the company you work for. And it will show you step by step how to implement EDM principles in your marketing campaign.

You really can't afford not to read this book. It is a virtual certainty that the process of EDM will increasingly affect your life in some way. If you are involved in a business of any kind, then the concepts and practical information detailed here will help you not only to cope with this marketing "revolution," but to profit from it as well.

I would like to specifically thank Janet Cunningham for her editorial assistance and, just as important, for much-appreciated moral support during the writing of this book.

1

ELECTRONIC DIRECT MARKETING: YOUR KEY TO SUCCESS

You are about to learn one of the most exciting and rewarding marketing techniques available today. Not only is it a technique that is already being used by some of the largest corporations in the world, but it is also successfully and increasingly being used by the small businessperson-entrepreneur with a product or service to sell. It is called Electronic Direct Marketing. Electronic Direct Marketing (EDM) is a technique that is relatively new, but it uses methods that have been successful for more than 100 years. What is new about the technique is that it combines the concept of direct marketing with the powerful and pervasive telecommunications industry: the electronic media of television, radio, and the telephone. This combination is proving so popular that Electronic Direct Marketing is not only the fastest growing form of marketing today; it also appears to be the direction of marketing in the 1980s and beyond.

ELECTRONIC DIRECT MARKETING DEFINED

The technique of EDM is quite familiar to all of us. We have all seen or heard commercials offering products for sale on television or radio that request us to respond by calling a phone number or mailing to an address. Or we may have been contacted by a telephone marketer offering to sell a product or service. We may have read about or participated in experiments involving computerized interactive shop-at-home services. We may even have been one of a growing number of consumers who have purchased one or more of the hundreds of products that are available through EDM channels. Whatever the form of EDM we may be most familiar with, the following general definition holds true for all variations of EDM:

> *Electronic Direct Marketing is an interactive system of marketing that uses one or more advertising media, including one or more of the electronic media, to effect a measurable response and/or transaction independent of a retail outlet.*

Instead of a retail outlet, the transaction is completed through the mail, through a salesperson, or through the follow-up use of more detailed literature that more fully describes the product or service.

GROWTH OF EDM

No matter who you are or what business you are in, the businessperson who survives is the one who can adapt to changing market conditions. In today's turbulent business environment the profitable marketing of goods and services can frequently be a risky proposition. In addition to traditional competitive factors, businesses are confronted with such problems as persistent inflation and recessionary cycles. To combat these forces, it is imperative that marketers have tight control over the marketing dollars they spend. An increasing number of businesspeople—from the smallest entrepreneur to the marketing managers of the largest corporations—are taking a hard look at the marketing options open to them and are channeling their marketing expenditures into those marketing techniques that offer them the best opportunities for tracking the "usefulness" of those dollars. They are choosing techniques that are both *cost accountable* and *cost effective*. Because EDM fulfills these needs of cost accountability *and* cost effectiveness, at times to a dramatically successful degree, and because it is available to businesses of almost all sizes, EDM has become today's fastest growing merchandising technique.

Even though EDM had been used with some success since the early days of the electronic media, it was not until the early 1970s that the idea of tying direct marketing methods to the electronic media really gained momentum. Today some estimates have pegged the current overall growth of EDM at three to five times that of regular business. The Direct Mail Marketing Association estimates that direct response advertising expenditures for the electronic media are now nearly $15 *billion* a year and rising rapidly.

The growth of EDM is also reflected in the amount of the available inventory of commercial time that is being devoted to EDM. For example, it is not uncommon to see many independent television and radio stations devote as much as 50 percent of their time to EDM promotions.

The fastest growing of the EDM areas is telephone direct marketing: using the telephone to (1) capture orders generated from other direct response media, or (2) to directly contact potential customers to sell a product or concept or to produce leads. Current estimates place total telephone marketing expenditures at more than $13 billion, an amount more than four times greater than that spent for direct response newspaper advertising, and an amount nearly as great as the $14 billion spent for direct mail (both of which usually also carry a telephone number for response). Every day telephone salespeople place more than 7 million calls and sell more than $30 million worth of products, ranging from swimming pools to life insurance.

EDM HISTORY

The technique of EDM had its beginnings in the earliest days of the telecommunications industry. The telephone was probably the first of the electronic forms to be used for a direct sale. Insurance companies, for example, discovered they could save time and money by finding clients and selling them policies via the telephone.

The radio was used occasionally for EDM promotions. Probably the largest and most noticeable users of EDM in the thirties and forties were the radio evangelists. Listeners who liked what they heard were encouraged to dig deeply into their pockets for a course, or a booklet, or some religious trinket. It is not known exactly how successful these evangelists were in their time, but many are still active today, and many have switched to television, joined by other newer faces as well. These evangelists have survived and thrived on a national and international basis, some with memberships in the hundreds of thousands, dependent almost solely upon the income directly received from a congregation developed through the electronic media.

The early days of television saw sporadic use of this medium as a direct marketing tool. Television was mainly used as a general advertising stage for local retail outlets and later, as television went nationwide, as a medium for nationwide promotions of products sold through local retail outlets. There were times, however, when direct response promotions were successfully used. One of the earliest successes was the sale of an art course that before being sold on television was producing a grand total of $75 a month. The course was so well received on television that at the conclusion of the promotion one out of every fourteen television owners in America purchased the course!

Many of the early promotions on television were characterized by rapidfire narrations, almost unbelievable claims, and a predominance of gadgets, gizmos, and record albums, all packaged into a carnivallike atmosphere. Direct marketers found they could move their products in this way and stuck with these methods for many years. The company that gave us the chopper-grater salesman showing us 600 ways to slice a potato and a multitude of similar products grew into a multimillion-dollar corporation using these methods. In fact, the founder of this corporation actually began his career by selling gadgets at carnivals and fairs. Today marketers are still finding some success with these types of promotions, but the significant portion of today's direct marketing commercials is quite unlike what most of us have come to identify with EDM. These types of commercials also tend to come to mind because they have often been satirized in television and the press, probably justifiably so.

The advent of direct marketers who were more inclined to test their promotions in a more sophisticated and precise manner led to the discovery that their commercials were alienating a huge segment of potential consumers who would be inclined to purchase products via EDM if those products were presented using a different and more subtle approach. It was also eventually discovered that the buying public could be enticed to purchase a wider variety of products and services than those historically sold. When direct marketers refined their approaches to appeal to this wider market segment, and when they began to offer a wider variety of products and services through all three major EDM channels, EDM began to grow in virtual leaps and bounds.

CRITERIA FOR SUCCESS

EDM is not necessarily restricted to those individuals with years of experience and hundreds of thousands of dollars to spend. On the contrary, almost anyone can successfully use at least one of the EDM marketing channels, and money is not the primary factor in the ability to succeed. You can use the electronic media to market your product or idea even if your resources are limited. If you are serious about finding a way to start or expand your own business, EDM may be the most appropriate and profitable alternative for you.

1. It is crucial that you gain a fundamental understanding of EDM. This book will provide you with those fundamentals, and will also provide you with additional reference resources for your area of specific need.

2. You must have a product or idea that lends itself to EDM. As you will see, this is not necessarily a restrictive criterion, as nearly any product can be successfully direct-marketed via at least one of the electronic media.

3. You must be prepared to properly develop and test your commercial package. This book will teach you the basics of putting together a promotion, and then show you how to test it for profitability.

4. You must be prepared to make at least a moderate capital investment. Depending on the way you choose to begin, your initial dollar investment may be one third or even less of the amount required to start a traditional retail business. And once you've tested and found success in your promotion, this book will show you how to "roll out" your promotion to other market areas, in many cases without requiring a personal capital commitment beyond that of your original investment.

5. It is to your advantage if you have some sales skills. Research has shown that the most successful direct marketers are those who can get along well with others and who have the ability to sell things or concepts to others face-to-face.

6. As in any business, there is a direct correlation between the amount of effort you put into it and what you get out of it. And even though EDM has the potential to give back in much greater proportion than most methods of marketing, you must still be prepared to work for your success, have a penchant for persistence, and have an inner desire to succeed. This factor is so crucial to your success that later in this chapter we will be discussing the importance of commitment, and especially how it relates to the direct marketing environment.

Some Success Stories

The opportunity to make a large amount of money in a very short period of time is the desire of every businessperson. EDM is an avenue that may allow you to do just that. The right product combined with the right promotional approach can produce a veritable gold mine of profits.

How successful can you be? At the risk of making this sound like "How I Made a Million Dollars in Three Days in My Spare Time," I'll give you some examples that are representative of some successes involving EDM. Even though there are risks involved in EDM, as in any business, there is also the probability that you may have a hit on your hands. It's nice to know it's possible:

One Atlanta television station reported that a recent series of direct sales advertisements promoting a record album was broadcast intermittently over a forty-five-minute period. The incoming rush of orders put such a strain on telephone order takers that the station had to temporarily suspend further broadcast of the advertisement. When the smoke had cleared, the marketer had received more than 16,000 orders!

A church group attempting to raise funds on a limited promotional budget used $1,200 to create and buy time for an ad that asked for donations to their church. The response was a bit more than they had anticipated: more than $400,000 in one weekend!

In a recent marketing campaign, a company promoted a book using EDM in twelve market areas. Within ten days the company sold in excess of 700,000 copies!

Another company tried backing up their direct mailings to customers with telephone direct sales support. They reported a *700 percent* increase in sales over a similar promotion that did not use the telephone.

Of course, these examples are meant to illustrate the potential for dramatic returns when the electronic media are used for direct marketing. This is not to say that every promotion or product can be as successful. But with correct preparation, including following the steps in this book, your probability of a hit will increase significantly. And even if one of your promotions is a flop, the direct marketing methods that you will learn will enable you to pull out of or modify your promotion *before* you lose your shirt, not after.

ROADBLOCKS TO EDM ENTRY

Television, radio, and the telephone have become so commonplace (more than 97 percent of all United States households contain all *three* of them) that we tend to take them for granted. Yet the electronic media have an incredible influence on the way we think and the way we live. We have come to depend on the electronic media for our news, our entertainment, and for communication. Statistics show that we turn to the electronic media first for our information needs. More than 75 percent of us depend on television or radio as our primary news source. Even more amazing is the fact that the average family watches television six hours and thirteen minutes every day!

It is little wonder that direct marketers may have more than a passing interest in tapping the vast consumer gold mine found in the electronic media. Two factors, however, have in the past hindered entry of most marketers into this arena: (1) lack of any available training or documentation relating to the feasibility of EDM, and (2) misconceptions about the costliness of EDM.

Let's discuss each of these points. First, the bulk of direct marketing has historically been in the print media. Most marketers received their training in the print media, wrote copy, developed promotions, and gained all their experience in the print media. The electronic arena, at least psychologically, represented a switch into a field that was foreign to most direct marketers. Because the successful use of EDM does require some preparation, and because there were few with experience who could or would pass along their knowledge, most attempts at EDM were hit-or-miss at best. In addition, direct marketers found little reason to attempt a move into EDM in the first place, because little research or documentation was available that justified entry into an apparently risky and untested area.

There are few avenues to which the marketer can turn for learning the practical application of the EDM technique, especially in the area of television and radio direct response. Some periodicals occasionally include articles on some aspect of EDM. There are also a few well-written direct marketing books that may also be helpful in gaining some insight into the direct marketing process.

Other sources of information are local television and radio stations, and some advertising agencies. Most stations are not prepared to educate marketers about the "how to" of EDM but are good sources of information regarding purchasing time. In some cases they will be able to help you with commercial production. Advertising agencies proficient in EDM are few in number and located mainly on the East Coast and in Chicago. Unless you are a qualified client, most agencies will be reluctant to discuss with you their techniques or specific accomplishments.

MARKETING COSTS COMPARED

As direct marketers search for less expensive alternatives to the print media, the electronic arena is becoming the increasingly popular choice. This is because the costs of the various direct response media have risen disproportionately to the costs of electronic media time, thereby making the costs of electronic media surprisingly affordable. Of the three major electronic alternatives—telephone, radio, and television—television is frequently and mistakenly assumed to be an unaffordable luxury. Unfortunately, many direct marketers, and especially the smaller direct marketers, may not consider EDM a viable alternative because of a mistaken belief that a successful promotion would mean heavy commercial expense within highly rated, extremely expensive national network programs. This fear of exorbitant costs is in most cases unfounded. Direct response marketers have learned that high ratings and highly priced nationwide ads do not necessarily create profitable returns. In fact, direct marketers have discovered that there is usually an inverse relationship between low ratings and direct response profits. In other words, advertising within the lowest-rated programs increases the chances for enhanced customer response. And of course, the greater the response, the higher the probability of a promotion's being successful.

When a viewer is watching (or listening to) a program in which his or her interest is high, it's difficult to get that viewer to run to the telephone, or to grab a pencil or paper to write a telephone number or address. But when that viewer is watching a program to which his or her level of attentiveness is low, your commercial has a higher probability of generating a customer response.

The purchase of time within lower-rated television and radio programs translates into a much lower cost per commercial than one might expect. In some metropolitan areas, for example, sixty-second commercials within a negotiated package of time may cost less than $40 apiece. In some cases it is possible to use the per inquiry method of obtaining television and radio time, whereby you pay nothing until you sell your products.

The fact that television and radio time can be relatively inexpensive is good news to direct marketers who are facing rising costs in other areas of direct marketing. Direct mail costs, for example, have skyrocketed in the last decade. The average cost of direct mailing pieces (postage, paper, printing, and so on) was $120 per thousand in 1970. By 1975, this cost had risen 50 percent to $180 per thousand. A statistical sample of television costs in this same time period showed that these costs had risen only 7 percent. Today's direct mailing costs can be well over $300 per thousand. Television and radio costs, on the other hand, have remained relatively stable, especially in the lower-rated programs, where it has been historically difficult to sell advertising time at a premium.

The state of the economy is one major factor in holding down these rates. Because television and radio rates are based on supply and demand, these rates can vary from season to season. Not only do yearly cyclical cost trends develop as a consequence of changing viewing audiences, but costs also reflect changing economic patterns. During periods of healthy economic growth, demand for available electronic media time increases, and the cost of time also increases to reflect this higher demand. During a sluggish economy, many businesses tend to cut back on their advertising expenditures, creating a situation of excess supply for local stations. In order for these stations to fill unused time, lower negotiated rates for direct marketers become more available. The direct marketer can take advantage of these lower rates to reduce per order costs.

These lower rates offer an additional degree of opportunity to the direct response marketer. Direct mail costs, for example, tend to remain high no matter how sluggish the economy. Postage costs, a major component of direct mail costs, are relatively fixed, at least on the down side, as are printing and other component costs. The lowered costs and the increased availability of commercial time during sluggish economic periods are therefore particularly attractive to the direct marketer who is looking for a hedge against cyclical cost-versus-return variables.

Another area of direct marketing being hit by increased costs is direct sales. The cost of a business sales call, for example, has risen as dramatically as direct mail costs. According to a study by McGraw-Hill, published in *Fact Book on Direct Response Marketing*, by the end of 1976, the cost of one type of sales call, the industrial sales call made in person, was about $80. A year later that cost had risen to $95. Today's cost is nearly $200. And considering the fact that it takes an average of 4.3 calls to complete a sale, the cost per sale is obviously much higher.

In contrast, the cost of an industrial sales call completed over the telephone has not increased significantly over the past decade. The use of the "800" outward WATS (wide area telephone service) line, where the marketer pays a discount for a block of telephone time rather than for each individual call, has been one factor that has kept the average *total* cost per call under $8. Other types of telephone sales calls can cost significantly less than half that. And for order-taking purposes, where a customer calls in his or her order via an inward "800" WATS line (which is toll-free to the customer), the cost per call averages less than $3.

Telephone sales programs are beginning to be instituted by many businesses throughout the United States. National Steel Service Center, Inc., for example, credits a major part of its 400 percent increase in sales volume in less than seven years to its telephone sales program. Another company, National Weather Corporation, reports that its telephone marketing program doubled the company's twenty-year volume during the program's first two years.

THE DIMENSIONS OF EDM

Unlike the print media or regular retail methods, the electronic media add the dimensions of sound and action. Television, radio, and the telephone each have unique attributes that can be used to generate excitement in a product or idea by making the product or idea "come alive." Television, for example, allows a consumer to see or hear a product in action; a record can be played, or benefits of another product can be colorfully and graphically portrayed, and verbal explanations can be given. Even though radio and the telephone cannot show what a product looks like, the word picture that is presented when products are explained verbally can stimulate the imagination and create action.

The telephone also has some unique attributes. Although direct mail, for example, may go unread, more people will listen and participate in a telephone conversation. With the telephone a two-way rapport can be established, and objections can be met and overcome.

Direct marketers using the print media have always faced the challenge of making the consumer aware of their products and have devised countless ways to entice the consumer to at least read their advertising copy. Even with these attempts to interest the consumer, a significant number of offerings never are read, or in the case of direct mail, the envelope may never even be opened. The offering is then thrown away without giving the marketer the opportunity to explain a product that the consumer may really want or need. In a sense, the electronic media can be thought of as an envelope that has already been opened. The commercial offering, whether it be via television, radio, or telephone, is at least presented to the consumer. If consumers then decide that the product is not for them, they will simply turn off their attention, in the case of television and radio, or with the telephone will simply say "no, thank you" and hang up. Even though there may be other factors that will spell the success or failure of your promotion, at least you have been given the opportunity to tell your story to the consumer.

One additional benefit of the electronic media relates to the comparative degree of competition for consumer attention that an ad may have at any one time. If you place your direct response ad in a magazine, for example, you may be placed on a page that contains a number of ads. Even though these ads may be unrelated to your product, they nevertheless compete for the consumer's attention, increasing the probability that your ad will go unnoticed. On the other hand, within the electronic media, advertisements are presented one at a time, allowing the consumer to consider each ad individually.

Summary of Important Points

EDM is the fastest growing of all marketing techniques. EDM is cost accountable and cost effective.

There is an inverse relationship between levels of customer attentiveness to a program and the response to a commercial.

Refinement of EDM ads has attracted a new consumer audience.

EDM can be used by almost any kind and size of business to promote almost any kind of product or service.

Advertising and marketing costs of other direct response media have risen disproportionately to EDM costs.

The electronic media provide unique attention-getting and motivational tools to generate consumer response in an EDM promotion.

2

WHY DIRECT MARKETING?

Because direct marketing is tied so intimately to the EDM process, it is important to understand how and why direct marketing contributes toward making EDM an effective technique.

The objective of direct marketing is to derive a direct response from the consumer, either in the form of a direct sale or by establishing a lead for later follow-up through more detailed literature or through direct sales contact.

It could probably be argued that the direct marketing process has been with us since man began to trade. In early civilizations people tended to complete their transactions in a direct sales environment, taking their goods or services directly to consumers. Since that time, of course, the field of direct marketing has grown, not only in size, but in sophistication as well. The following is a brief review of the major forms of direct marketing. We will be referring to them throughout the book.

Direct Mail: The objective of direct mail is to elicit a direct response from a consumer, based on a promotional package mailed to the consumer. The promotional package may contain copy for one product or several, or the package may be included as an insert in a bill. For example, major oil companies such as Exxon, Mobil, and Arco are finding it profitable to include in their monthly billing statements advertising for products that can be purchased by return mail. Usually a direct marketer, called a syndicator, will prepare the insert and pay the companies a percentage of each product sold.

Another popular form of direct mail is called co-op direct mail. With co-op direct mail a marketer (syndicator) will prepare a mailing that will promote one or a number of his or her products. The marketer will then "rent" space in the mailing to other direct marketers. Marketers who rent or share their space with others can generally cover their costs of preparation and mailing, thereby reducing the risk involved in the promotion.

Direct mail marketing has evolved into a highly sophisticated and precise science, increasingly utilizing complex measurement techniques to assist marketers in their work. The increased accuracy that these tools have given them has allowed the direct mail industry to remain competitive and profitable in the face of continually rising costs.

This sophistication has kept direct mail at the forefront of the direct response industry. Its growth rate is 15 percent, twice that of retail business. Direct mail now accounts for about 30 *billion* of the 106 billion pieces of mail sent each year.

Catalogs: The first catalog designed to elicit response by mail was prepared by Montgomery Ward in 1872. Shortly thereafter the Sears-Roebuck catalog made its debut. The catalog was a godsend to those customers who lived far from any major population center.

Today hundreds of different catalogs are produced for every manner of product and service category. Ambassador and Sunset House are two companies that offer hundreds of products via direct mail in catalog form. Every year these firms mail millions of catalogs to past and potential customers. Ambassador, by the way, also uses television direct response to promote many of their products, and to gain new customer names to whom they can mail their catalogs.

Most of the major department stores now use some form of catalog or direct mail promotion within their marketing mix. For example, according to *Advertising Age*, department and specialty stores with annual sales of $75 million or more generally issue six to twenty catalogs each year, with circulations ranging from 100,000 to a million. Typical department stores during the Christmas season produce 15 percent or more of their total volume through telephone- and mail-generated orders.

Department stores are also finding that a well-organized direct marketing program can offer a return on investment substantially above that of normal retail margins. Doreen McCurley, vp–direct response for Bloomingdale's, says that their direct marketing operation enjoys an ROI ten times greater than the return on its stores. They anticipate a 40 percent growth in direct marketing sales for 1982–83.

Space Advertising: Space advertising was the first form of mail-order marketing. Early newspaper ads invited us to respond through the mail to a multitude of products ranging from mink stoles to medicine water. Today, space advertising includes mail-order ads placed in magazines, newspapers, and even paperback books. These ads may be in the form of a classified ad, or may use a full page or more to describe a product or products. An address, coupon, and, or, phone number is usually included in the ad for customer response.

Inserts: Inserts, also called preprints, can be index-sized cards or newspaper-sized advertising supplements that are inserted in magazines and newspapers. These inserts are bound or loosely inserted into the periodical and tend to be more noticeable than space advertising when the periodical is opened. The consumer tendency to handle or adjust these inserts has been found to contribute to consumer response. The index-sized cards are frequently used by publishers to advertise subscription renewals to their publications.

Miscellaneous Print Media: The forms that direct marketing can take are only limited by the imagination of the marketer. Marketers have found success by putting ads on cereal boxes, shopping bags, film envelopes, milk cartons; in short, almost anything that can "hold" an ad has been used for direct response.

Two minor forms of direct response (not minor, of course, to those marketers who derive their primary source of income from them) are "take-ones" and matchbooks. Take-ones are usually index-sized cards positioned next to a poster that advertises a product or service. The consumer is encouraged to take one of the cards, which may contain more product information and an address or phone number for response. Many times these cards are post cards with postage prepaid.

Matchbooks are a popular medium for products such as address labels, correspondence courses, insurance policies, and stamps. The inside of the matchbook makes a natural coupon for the product offer. Returns can be slow with a matchbook-based promotion. Usually, 20 percent of returns come in within the first six months, 75 percent within the first year.

Direct Selling: This personal direct marketing of goods or services is usually independent of a retail outlet. Direct sales also includes what is commonly known as door-to-door selling. The Avon Company, for example, sells more products door-to-door than any other company in the United States.

Direct Marketing in the Electronic Media: This marketing method is what this book is all about. As we will see, EDM utilizes the same concepts that make direct marketing in other forms successful.

It is important to keep in mind the various media options that are open to you. It is a rare product that can continually be successful in one medium only. For example, you may saturate the target market available to your initial medium. Or you may find that a combination of two or more media will work better for you. EDM can be used in conjunction with these other direct marketing forms to significantly increase response over what would be possible by using one method alone.

NEGATIVES AND POSITIVES OF THE DIRECT MARKETING INDUSTRY

From the consumer point of view, experience with direct marketing has not always been favorable. The direct marketing field has had more than its share of bad press. Who among us has not heard or read of the consumer who sends away for the product that never arrives, then finds that the marketer never intended to deliver the product, and the consumer can't get his or her money back because the marketer closed up shop and left no forwarding address.

One recent and somewhat famous example of a "marketer" defrauding the public comes to mind. This "marketer" advertised a digital watch quite heavily in several issues of *TV Guide* and other print media. The watch sold for about $20, which was a price that was a steal compared with other similar watches. A steal was exactly what it was, only it was the advertiser who did the stealing. After numerous complaints from consumers, it was discovered that there never were any watches, and the advertiser could not be found. He later was found in Mexico; much of the $1.7 million dollars he had collected was recovered and partial refunds were made.

Unfortunately, the sensationalization of these few bad apples has created a false impression of the entire direct marketing field. To many people the term "mail order" is synonymous with the term "con game." The actual truth, of course, is that there are far more reputable direct marketers than dishonest ones. Those who are dishonest do not last long. We now have potent laws designed to stop and punish dishonest mail-order marketers. Marketers who have intentions of being dishonest better not try it in the electronic media. These media, especially radio and television, are tightly controlled and regulated to insure against advertising fraud. In addition, most stations protect themselves by requiring marketers to provide an ample supply of the product being marketed before the station allows a direct response commercial to air.

No matter what the consumer perception of direct marketing may be, the statistics indicate what direct marketers have known for a long time: Every year consumers are spending more dollars than ever on directly marketed products and services. Direct marketing is now conservatively estimated to be a more-than-$150-*billion*-a-year industry, having grown more than 150 percent since 1975. The *Wall Street Journal* estimates the current growth rate of the direct-response industry to be up to 100 percent faster than that of regular business. Indications are that this growth will continue into the near future.

Why the huge consumer popularity with direct marketing? Consumers recognize, if only subconsciously, the advantages of convenience, economy, and selection that direct marketing offers them. With rising gasoline and transportation costs making it increasingly expensive to hop from one store to another, it certainly makes sense to purchase products and services by mail or telephone and have them delivered to your door. Some individuals are literally unable to go to stores because of age or physical handicap. For these individuals the availability of products through direct marketing channels is indeed a blessing.

The choice of products sold through direct marketing is virtually unlimited. There has probably never been a product or service that has not been sold by some form of direct marketing. The Texas-based Nieman-Marcus company, for example, distributes a catalog that contains some of the most exotic items imaginable. One year one of the items offered was a live elephant!

Direct marketing gives consumers access to products that local outlets may seldom stock. It is nice to know that you can buy fresh apples from Washington State or lobster from Maine through mail order.

Direct marketing can also offer the opportunity to purchase a product that may be available locally, but may be available at a much lower price through direct marketing.

ADVANTAGES FOR THE DIRECT MARKETER

For the direct marketer, and especially the budding entrepreneur with a product or idea to sell, direct-marketing methods can not only offer the ideal opportunity to test the profitability potential of their items, but also provide the solid basis for a successful business.

Although regular retail business has its place in society, and has historically been the most accepted way for people to start their own businesses, retail growth is rapidly losing ground to direct marketing. Most forms of direct marketing require no retail outlet, no huge warehouse of inventory and, most importantly, no huge capital outlay for assets that may not contribute to a particular product promotion—a capital outlay that may, because of the increased number of dollars involved, increase the financial risk of the marketing effort. Instead, the money that you allocate to a direct marketing effort is more highly concentrated in advertising and promotional costs. That investment is therefore tied more directly to a specific product or promotion, enhancing the effectiveness of every dollar you spend. Should you fail in your efforts, you basically lose only the difference between the cost of your campaign and the revenue it generated.

DIRECT MARKETING METHODOLOGIES

As has been mentioned, the factors of cost effectiveness and cost accountability are important considerations to marketers as they attempt to maintain profitability and growth in a complex business environment. In addition to accountability and cost effectiveness, the direct-marketing method allows marketers the benefits of immediacy, measurability, and selectivity. These concepts are best explained by discussing an example of one type of direct marketing campaign.

Let's assume that you are a direct marketer who has developed a line of videotape cassettes that contain "how to" lessons and demonstrations ranging from tennis lessons to cooking demonstrations, all taught by experts in their fields. You know that you have a quality product, but you also know that there are not all that many people out there who have the equipment necessary to play these videotapes. It is important then that the media you choose and whatever marketing or advertising methodology you choose must be geared toward reaching those most likely to purchase your product. More important, you want to reach the greatest number of people at the lowest possible cost per order and the highest possible return per order.

As a direct marketer, you have a choice of several methods and advertising approaches to reach your customers. For this promotion you choose a combination of electronic media and direct mail. You intend to send mailers to prospective customers and back up these mailings with telephone direct-sales calls.

Through a list broker you are able to purchase a list of names of consumers who have recently purchased videocassette recorders (VCRs). You then prepare a mailer that describes all of the reasons why the VCR owner can't live without this important addition to his or her videotape collection. You mail your offer to a sample of the owners on the list, wait a few days, and call all those to whom you mailed a package.

You are mailing and calling only a sample of the names on the list because you want to determine if extending or "rolling out" your promotion to the entire list will be worthwhile. The difference between profit and loss is normally very narrow in terms of percentage returns. An overwhelming direct-mail response, for example, may be

3 to 5 percent. If the mailing and telephone direct sales follow-up is successful, you can expand your mailing to all the customers on your list.

It is important that the eventual roll-out be continually monitored to ensure that satisfactory results are maintained. If you find that you are losing money, you may have to stop the promotion altogether and determine why the response was poor. Possibly by changing the copy of your mailing or your telephone script or by testing a new mailing package, you will find the one that is most profitable. Most marketers will test several variations of copy and price in their first test mailing, thus saving valuable time that can be used to promote the most successful package. You may find your product is unacceptable to the customer and you'll have to search for another product. You may want to try mailing to another list of customers. Or you may change the media mix you are using, perhaps using television EDM instead. (In fact, videocassettes are now being successfully direct-marketed on television.)

Let's now discuss the concepts that were listed before this example.

Selectivity: It would not make sense for a marketer to mail a product offering to just anyone with an address. In order to ensure a higher probability of a response, you chose the list of VCR owners, enabling you to target your promotion to those individuals most likely to purchase the product.

Immediacy: Returns from a direct-mail or telephone direct-sale promotion are relatively prompt. This immediate response lets a marketer assess his or her performance fairly quickly. Since time is money, the advantage of immediate returns means that a marketer can attack or regroup that much sooner and either profit or reduce costs. The electronic media provide returns that can be days, weeks, or even months faster than other forms of direct marketing in the print media. In many cases this time difference can spell the difference between a successful or unsuccessful promotion.

Measurability: The measurement techniques that the direct-response method provides make it possible to pinpoint fairly precisely which of a number of test promotions are most successful. Then, based on the day-to-day feedback from response or lack thereof in the roll-out, the marketer is able to continually track his or her progress.

Cost Accountability and Cost Effectiveness: Direct response methods provide the marketer with the tools to quickly and precisely assess performance. Direct response makes it possible for marketers to *account* for costs and tie these costs very closely to the products or services they sell. Through the control direct response provides, a campaign can be adjusted to take advantage of the most profitable marketing approach, or it can be modified or deleted in those areas that are weakest. By directing marketing expenditures and efforts into those areas that will provide the highest return, the direct marketer increases the *cost effectiveness* of every dollar spent.

ARE YOU A MARKETER OR AN ADVERTISER?

It is important to make a distinction between what we know as "regular" advertising and direct-response marketing. The difference can be stated as follows: The regular or general advertiser is satisfied with making an impression. The direct-response advertiser must stimulate immediate action.

In direct-response advertising a direct marketer attempts to make each ad self-supporting. That is, each ad must not only be able to cover the cost of its commercial time; it must also contribute a portion of its sales revenues to the cost of producing the ad and to any overhead costs, provide for the cost of the product or service offered, and still provide a profit. Each ad then stands alone every time it is presented. If it cannot stand alone, it must be modified or replaced.

In order to show that it can stand alone, each ad must have a mechanism within it that lets it "produce" by itself. The two most common mechanisms that allow a marketer to see how each ad is doing are the response channels of the telephone and the address. It is the telephone and the address that provide the direct marketer with information that general advertising cannot give.

General advertising does not usually contain an inherent direct measurement tool that lets an advertiser monitor each ad's specific performance. General advertisers can only hope that the ad that was developed from a preliminary and subjective analysis of the market will stimulate sales in some way. The hoped-for stimulation will usually not necessarily be apparent until after an entire ad promotion is in full swing or ended and all dollars are spent. Even then, it is difficult to tie advertising expenditures directly to product sales. Marketing managers are well aware that quite frequently millions of dollars are spent on advertising promotions that produce little or no appreciable change in sales, to the consternation of businesspeople and to the profit, at least in the short run, of the advertising agency.

Regular retail advertising has its place, of course, as does institutional advertising designed to promote customer awareness of a company or image. But it is the small businessperson particularly, and the large corporation increasingly, who cannot afford to spend money in this way. If you are a small businessperson, you will out of necessity be well advised to use that marketing or advertising technique that tells you exactly how your dollars are performing, especially since you probably have limited resources to begin with. The greater the extent to which you can use direct-response techniques within your ads, the better you will know the true effect of the dollars you are risking.

DIRECT SALE AND DIRECT LEAD EDM

In EDM, as in other forms of direct marketing, a consumer response is converted into a sale in one of two ways. The first is the direct sale. In a direct sale a customer response is converted into a sale directly from an EDM ad or sales call. No further follow-up is necessary. The customer response is the sale. The direct sale can therefore be thought of as a one-step process. Generally the direct sale or one-step process is used in cases where the consumer will be likely to purchase on impulse. This means that the product offered will generally be familiar to the consumer or will be moderately priced. Some familiar examples of direct sale EDM include record offers, magazine subscription offers, books, cosmetics, and exercise accessories; this includes anything the consumer perceives as being a low risk and worth the gamble of ordering based on limited information.

In contrast to direct-sale EDM is direct-lead EDM. Direct-lead EDM is the process of generating customer responses (leads) that can later be followed up and converted into sales. The follow-up involves use of the same or, more generally, another medium such as detailed brochures, or a direct-sales call, either in person or by telephone. Direct-lead EDM can therefore be thought of as a two-step process. Generally, direct-lead EDM is used in cases where a consumer would hesitate to purchase on the spur of the moment. Some examples of direct-lead EDM include insurance, technical or business school offers, and high-priced items.

Your choice of using a one-step or a two-step process is dependent upon (1) the nature of the business you are in; (2) the type of product or products you will be marketing; (3) the costs or availabilities of commercial time; and (4) your ability and experience in using a multimedia approach.

An insurance company would find it difficult to sell policies directly through the one-step process. A consumer would of course balk at purchasing a policy unless he or she had more details regarding the policy. In addition, an insurance company probably already has an able sales force available to follow up with the details. Because of these reasons this type of company may find that a direct-lead approach is the most appropriate choice.

If you happen to be offering a number of products at one time, direct-lead EDM would be the best approach to use. One direct marketer is successfully using the two-step process on television to sell a line of men's "Big and Tall" clothing. Because it takes much longer than one or two minutes to show an entire line of men's clothes, the commercials are designed to arouse consumer interest in the line. The consumer is then invited to call or write for a free catalog that contains pictures and descriptions of each item. The catalog then becomes the vehicle by which the response is converted into a sale.

Another common reason for using direct-lead EDM is related to the price of the product being offered. A higher priced product will naturally require a follow-up conversion effort, unless the product is an obviously exceptional buy.

Another reason for using direct-lead EDM has to do with media cost. Many direct-sale EDM commercials tend to be ninety to 120 seconds in length. This length can at times be more difficult to obtain than a sixty-second commercial, especially on network-affiliated stations that normally split their spots into thirty- and sixty-second segments. In order to have a better opportunity to obtain commercial time, and also to take advantage of the reduced cost of the sixty-second commercial, a marketer may elect to convert to a direct-lead format.

Of course, the use of the direct-lead method assumes you are prepared to follow up on responses in some way. To the extent that you are not now prepared to follow up with additional literature or sales force, it will be important to allow for the additional cost and effort that the direct-lead approach will require.

The term *lead* can also be thought of in a different manner. Both direct-sale EDM and direct-lead EDM can be used to accumulate customer names. These names, which can be thought of as leads, can become extremely valuable to you as your business grows. You can use these names in a number of different ways, including selling them to others as a list, or using the list to sell other products or services.

The list you build also gives you an opportunity to expand beyond the electronic media into other areas of direct response, such as direct mail. Names may be so valuable to a marketer that he or she may initially sell products at a loss through EDM or other channels just to be able to add names to the list for later use.

SUPPORT EDM

Direct marketers are always looking for ways to increase customer response from a promotion. Varying copy, changing the target audience, or any number of other modifications may help to increase response.

But no matter what the change, there comes a point when the apparent maximum response rate has been reached. Any change that will significantly increase this response rate at an incremental cost at or below that of the original cost per response or cost per conversion is a desirable addition to a direct marketer's arsenal of response-enhancing alternatives. A new technique, called support EDM, does just that. Support EDM is the use of television, radio, or the telephone to increase the response of a direct-advertising campaign in another direct-response medium, such as direct-mail or space advertising. Direct-support differs from direct-lead and direct-sale EDM in that the electronic media are used as assistors to another form of direct response, rather than as primary direct-sale or direct-lead tools. The electronic media are in most cases considered to be secondary to the main direct-response promotion because the electronic media are used to create response in the primary medium. When television or radio are used for support, the response comes from the primary medium that is supported. When the telephone is used for support, the response can be either from the primary medium or from the telephone, where the sale can be completed directly.

The application of support EDM has been with us for many years. More than twenty-five years ago *Readers' Digest* launched a radio campaign urging listeners to be sure to look in their mailboxes for a subscription offer. Today the largest users of support EDM include insurance companies, book and magazine publishers, and record companies. Publisher's Clearing House, for example, advertises its sweepstakes-oriented direct-mail campaign on television. Columbia Records and Tapes, Time-Life Books, and National Home Life Insurance also have found success with support EDM.

In many cases the effect of electronic support can be quite dramatic. Some advertisers have reported an increase in response rates of up to 50 percent, using only 5 to 10 percent of the total advertising budget. One researcher (Levy, 1977) found that the backing up of newspaper preprints (inserts) with television advertising increased their effectiveness by 95 percent and reduced the cost of acquiring a response by 41 percent.

Even more encouraging are the results that can be achieved by using telephone support to back up direct-mail promotions. Telephone support has been shown to increase response to a direct mailing by an *average* of 300 to 500 percent over that of a direct mailing alone (Murray, 1978). We have already mentioned that one marketer reported an increase of more than 700 percent.

Reports like these are exciting for direct marketers and certainly justify a look at the possibilities of using support EDM for your product or business.

The mechanics of implementing support EDM will not be the same as those utilized in direct-sale and direct-lead EDM when television and radio are used for support. This is because unlike direct-lead and direct-sale EDM, which generally find success with spot advertising buys on programs with low levels of attentiveness, support EDM follows the rules of general consumer advertising. These rules include learning to target your advertising as precisely as possible to the consumers you have contacted through the primary medium. It is important to gain a fundamental understanding of these rules and differences in order to ensure your successful use of the support EDM technique.

YOUR SUCCESS OR FAILURE— SOME CAVEATS

It is appropriate to interject a few points here about direct-marketing business start-ups and failures. If you are a budding entrepreneur about to make your initial foray into the business world, the odds against your succeeding are incredibly high. The Small Business Administration estimates that for every ten businesses that are begun today, only one will still be in operation five years from now. More specifically, the odds against your success in the direct marketing field are even higher. It has been estimated that almost 98 percent of all mail order start-up attempts will fail within the same five-year time period. These odds make it appear that the direct marketing field is a hopeless cause. And yet, incredibly enough, the direct marketing and mail-order field is by far the most popular area of all businesses that are begun. Every year millions of dollars are spent on mail-order instruction alone. And direct-marketing/direct-mail start-ups are more than ten times more prevalent than the next most popular form of business start-up.

In spite of the immense odds against them, why do people continue to march to the direct marketing field like lemmings to the sea? Most individuals are attracted to direct marketing because of the mistaken belief that direct marketing is an arena where it is possible to get rich quick. Part of the problem with the continuance of this belief is the fact that most direct marketing books fail to stress, and in some cases fail to mention, that to succeed in direct marketing can be as difficult, if not more so, as it is to succeed in any other type of business endeavor.

Unfortunately the direct-marketing business does not discriminate among entrants based on the degree of commitment each may have. One of the main reasons why so many direct response businesses fail is because of the relative ease with which a person can begin a direct-response business. The fact that a direct-response business can be started with a relatively small amount of capital may subconsciously create a correspondingly small psychological commitment. Many beginners therefore do not put forth the effort required to learn and to work for their success. The truth is that any business endeavor, no matter how small the business or the capital commitment, will require an intense commitment of time, thought, and effort.

The point we are trying to make here is that in spite of the level of monetary commitments your business may require, keep your psychological commitment high. The factors of desire, persistence, and the will to succeed, combined with the knowledge this book and experience will give you, will most certainly and significantly increase the probability of your succeeding at EDM. But if you approach the business of EDM in the same way that most people approach other forms of direct response, the only success you will have is that you will succeed at failing. End of lecture.

Summary of Important Points

EDM may not be the entire solution for every marketing need, but in many cases it is the increasingly better choice for marketers because (1) costs are steadily rising in other marketing media; (2) EDM may have lower capital requirements than many forms of retail business; (3) EDM provides you with the necessary tools to track and control the performance of your marketing dollars; and (4) EDM offers the increased potential for more dramatic and profitable returns than other forms of marketing.

The choice of EDM can in addition supplement or round out a marketer's total marketing approach. The most successful marketers are those who are flexible enough to make wise use of all media forms and marketing techniques available to them. Marketers who depend on one medium or marketing approach for their success will more often than not see their businesses eventually decline. The more alternatives you can take advantage of, the greater your opportunity to succeed where others may fail.

3

TELEVISION EDM

The growth rate of television EDM over the last decade has been dramatic. In 1969, the Television Bureau of Advertising, Inc. reported that television EDM advertising expenditures were approximately $22 million. Today, aided by the introduction of the telephone and the "800" number as a response vehicle, as well as by an increasing consumer acceptance of television EDM as a shopping alternative, annual television EDM advertising expenditures have grown (according to the Direct Mail/Marketing Association: *Fact Book on Direct Response Marketing*, 1982) to more than $350 million. And the continued growth of television EDM shows no signs of slowing. On the contrary, all signs point to an accelerated growth rate that will surpass that of the last decade. Let's take a look at a few of the reasons why.

Television Is Pervasive. The television is everywhere. The 1982 *Television Fact Book* reports that there is now an average of two television sets for every family in the United States, thus making us the first country in the world to achieve such a (dubious?) distinction. We've already mentioned that the majority of us rely on the television as a primary source of information and entertainment. Average family viewing time, already substantial at more than six hours per day, is also on the increase.

Television Is Powerful. Television is without a doubt the most powerful of all direct marketing media, especially when it is combined with the telephone for immediate response. Within sixty to 120 seconds we can contact thousands of potential customers and ask them to buy or find out more about our product. Probably the best example of the kind of response that can be generated by EDM is the annual Jerry Lewis Muscular Dystrophy Telethon. In less than twenty-four hours, the 1983 Telethon generated almost *$30 million* in donations, with the vast majority of the money being pledged via the telephone.

Television Has Mass-Market and Audience-Specific Flexibility. Television EDM is ideally suited for products that have appeal for the mass market, but it can also be used effectively for almost any product. Products that have application to specific or very narrow audiences continue to do well with television EDM because (1) audiences can be targeted by purchasing spots that are adjacent to programs watched by the target audience; (2) the audience cost per thousand of television is much lower than any other direct marketing medium except radio; and (3) the measurability of EDM lets you test your promotion for effectiveness, and then lets you monitor and fine tune that promotion during your roll-out.

Television Opens up New Opportunities. The rapid growth of cable television and the proliferation of hundreds of new television channels are opening up new opportunities for the direct marketer. In addition, the testing and growth of two-way interactive technology is paving the way for the day when our televisions will be connected to a central computer. We will have access to data bases containing hundreds of thousands of pages of information. Among the hundreds of potential applications of the new technology will be our ability to select and order products and services with the push of a few buttons.

COST PER THOUSAND COMPARISON

One reason for the strong appeal of television among direct marketers is its lower cost per thousand relative to other direct-response media. Newspaper inserts, for example, can cost more than $30 per thousand. Direct-mail costs can range as high as $300 to $400 per thousand. Television costs, on the other hand, can average $3 per thousand or less. This cost differential means, assuming cost per order requirements remain the same for a particular product, that fewer orders are required to break even on a promotion in television than in another direct response medium such as direct mail.

Let's look at a simple example of the differences in response necessary to maintain a satisfactory cost per order in two different media—direct mail versus television.

How many orders need to be generated in each medium to maintain an acceptable cost per order of $8?

TWO SAMPLE PROMOTIONS:

Direct mail: 100,000 mailings at $350 per thousand = (350) (100) = $35,000. In order to achieve a cost per order of $8, the promotion must generate 35,000/8 = 4,375 orders, or 43.7 orders per thousand.

Television: Assuming it will cost $3,000 to reach 1,000,000 television households (using an average cost per thousand of $3), the promotion needs to generate 3000/8 = 375 orders, or 0.37 orders per thousand.

As you can see, the difference in response requirements between the two media is substantial. But don't let the numbers mislead you. Response depends a great deal on the product, the offer, and the audience. In a normal promotion, direct mail will outpull television on an order per thousand basis, which is why, even though the numbers favor television, direct mail continues to be a popular direct response medium. But the numbers also show what more and more television EDM marketers are discovering: a well-produced, thoroughly tested EDM promotion has the potential to be more profitable in television than in any other medium. This is because risk can be minimized. Returns do not need to be as high as they do in other media to break even, and, because the break-even point is relatively low, your opportunity to maximize profits if a hit develops is increased.

QUALITY

Consumer perception of the quality of the direct response commercial has, at least in past years, been below that of general television advertising. Some types of EDM commercials, although attention getting and profitable, are extremely obnoxious to many viewers. The fast-talking "chopper grater" salesman, for example, has often been parodied on television. This author's favorite parody occurred a few years ago on the television show, *Saturday Night Live*. Dan Aykroyd, a cast member who regularly mimicked the EDM commercial, took the opportunity one night to offer for "sale" the Bass-O-Matic blender. In front of a live audience, the fast-talking Aykroyd dropped a bass into a madly churning blender filled with water. The bass, of course, was instantly transformed into a disgusting-looking bass "drink," which Aykroyd's assistant, Laraine Newman, downed with relish.

The shoddy-looking, cheaply produced commercial has created something of a bad name for itself and may have helped to create a negative consumer attitude toward all types of television advertising. A recent survey polled consumers regarding their attitudes toward several direct marketing advertising media: television, direct mail, magazines, newspapers, and radio. The results of the poll showed that the respondents felt that television was not only the least honest and trustworthy of the media; they also felt it was the most irritating and annoying.

The quality of EDM commercials has increased dramatically over the last few years. There are several reasons for this. First of all, as larger corporations jump into an EDM field that was once the domain of small, sometimes one-person, operations, the budgets being allocated to commercial production have increased. The increased monies allocated to production allow directors and producers more flexibility in content and style than was possible in the past. Secondly, the proliferation of support advertising, which is more impression-type advertising than that of direct-sale and direct-lead EDM advertising, has attracted into the field advertising agencies who are more adept at creating the high-budget, slickly produced commercials found in general advertising. The resulting commercials are a blend of high-quality production techniques and direct marketing fundamentals. Lastly, and probably most important, rather than assuming that the kind of EDM commercial that was effective in the past will continue to be effective in the future, an increasing number of direct marketers are testing their promotions more thoroughly before rolling them out. They are finding that a large segment of the target market that was in the past "turned off" by the stereotypical direct marketing promotion is now responding enthusiastically to more subtle, better-quality EDM promotions.

IT'S NOT AS EXPENSIVE AS YOU THINK

As we mentioned in the previous chapter, many direct marketers unfamiliar with the application of television to direct response tend to dismiss television EDM out of hand because of mistaken estimates of the potential cost involved in rolling out a promotion. This fear is in most cases unfounded because, rather than advertising in expensive national network spots, the direct marketer does the bulk of his or her advertising within or adjacent to lower-rated programs on a local spot basis. These advertisers have found that high ratings and highly priced nationwide ads do not necessarily create profitable returns.

Most direct-response advertising is broadcast on independent local television stations, although an increasing amount of advertising is being carried on network affiliate stations. Local independent stations are popular with direct marketers because the inventories (commercial time) of independent stations are comprised entirely of local spot availabilities. Local independent stations also are able to offer the longer 120-second spots, a common, useful length for direct-response commercials. Network affiliates, on the other hand, do not have as much local spot inventory, and the availability of 120-second spots is more limited.

One advantage of spot television is its flexibility. Spot purchases allow the direct marketer to choose particular markets at particular times. For example, a marketer may have several different products being promoted simultaneously in several different markets, concentrating advertising for each product in the specific markets that produce the most successful returns.

Many direct marketers consider cost per response to be the most important factor in purchasing and measuring response from television spots. A more significant cost indicator, however, is cost per sale (or conversion). For example, a direct-lead ad may produce a $2 cost per inquiry, but if only 10 percent of these are converted into sales, the cost per conversion would be $20. Thinking of a sale in terms of cost per conversion provides for a more uniform analysis of direct sales and direct lead ads because cost per conversion is the end result of both the one-step and two-step process. Another advantage in the use of cost per conversion is that it forces a direct marketer to think in terms of quality rather than the quantity of leads that are produced. It should also be remembered that cost per response or cost per sale should take into consideration product returns or refusals. The percentage of returns and refusals can sometimes be quite high, and if allowances are not made for them, obvious problems could result.

RATINGS AND RESPONSE

In most television EDM promotions it has been found that the level of consumer response to an ad is inversely related to the levels of attentiveness to television programs. The less attentive the viewer is to the program, the higher the response. This is why so many direct response commercials are adjacent to game shows, old movies, talk shows, reruns of situation comedies or other similar programs, and next to late-night programs.

Television EDM marketers are heavy users of television spot discount prices. These discounts include preemptive spots, run-of-station, and various package deals that differ from station to station. Generally, the use of these lower-cost spot prices enables the advertiser to bring down the overall cost per order.

Prices for spots are based on audience ratings and demand. The higher the rating and the higher the demand, the steeper the spot price. Spot costs on most stations are structured to increase as less and less inventory becomes available for purchase. The negotiated discounts, especially run-of-station and direct-response package deals, are usually available within the lower-rated programs. These lower-rated programs tend to have lower levels of attentiveness, an ideal situation for the direct-response marketer.

A preemptible spot is not a guaranteed spot and can be bumped at any time by an advertiser who pays the more expensive non-preemptible rate for the same time slot. The preemptible spot may be cancelled, or, depending on your agreement with the station, may be aired in a different time slot at a later date. Run-of-station means that the advertiser can purchase a certain number of spots per week, usually preemptible, and the station will run them when and where it pleases within the constraints of negotiated time periods. For example, you may be able to purchase a run-of-station package that will air spots any time within the time periods of Monday through Friday, 9 A.M. to 1 P.M. Other run-of-station packages give stations the leeway to air spots between station sign-on and sign-off.

Many advertisers utilize run-of-station packages, not only because their commercials will be run within programs with a low level of attentiveness, but also because they can gain demographic flexibility at less cost than they could with spots that are guaranteed. For example, a large number of product offerings during the day appeal to women and children. Advertisers know that the television viewing audiences in the morning and afternoon hours are predominantly women and children. A direct marketer can therefore take advantage of the lowest rates possible, perhaps a run-of-station package from 9 A.M. to 1 P.M., and still be selective in the audience he or she is trying to reach. If the marketer wishes to be even more selective in reaching the target audience, it will be necessary to pay a higher spot price and advertise within or near specific programs.

An increasing number of stations, both independent and network, are making available time packages tailored specifically to the direct response marketer. Some stations, for example, offer special packages that allow the marketer to be program-specific and still take advantage of lower-than-normal rates. One West Coast independent station sells a package of spots that is preemptible until the Wednesday prior to the week of play, but is confirmed (nonpreemptible) after that day. There is a minimum purchase that must be made: ten "60s" or five "120s" per week. Sixty-second spots have priority over 120-second spots. The rates vary by time segment and length of commercial.

These special packages are usually offered during the first and third quarters of the year when it is difficult for many stations to sell all of their time at the highest nonpreemptible rates. Direct marketers may find it difficult to purchase discounted inventory in many markets during the second and fourth quarters, simply because these stations have little trouble selling their inventory then.

Some stations, especially network affiliates, have more than enough demand for their time and seldom offer discounted packages, even during historically slower parts of the year. One Spokane, Washington, network station, for example, only accepts two or three direct response advertisers on run-of-station packages during the first and third quarters. They do not offer discounted rates during the second and fourth quarters. The station requires a full thirteen-week commitment with a minimum of twenty 120-second spots, or its equivalent, per week. The marketer has no choice about commercial placement, which could be any time from sign-on until sign-off.

SPOT TELEVISION RATES AND DATA AND ARBITRON

The following resources are aids to purchasing spot time:

Spot Television Rates and Data, (STRD) is published by the Standard Rate and Data Service, Inc., in Skokie, Illinois. The STRD is essentially composed of (1) seventeen consumer market categories that include, for example, total television households in a market, consumer spendable income, total retail sales, and automotive store sales; (2) breakdowns of television market areas ranked in descending order based on size; and (3) the publication of the rate cards of all participating television stations.

These rate cards usually reflect the standard nonpreemptible and preemptible prices for each station and do not include run-of-station or special packages. For the determination of the availability of special rates, the advertiser must contact the station directly.

Another source that is an aid in purchasing spot time is *Arbitron,* a publication that breaks down program viewing audiences by size, age, and sex, all important considerations in maximizing target impact. A separate *Arbitron* is published for each television market, 122 in all.

USING THE COMPUTER TO TRACK SPOT PURCHASES

Frequently the biggest problem with spot television purchases is the difficulty of handling these purchases. To plan a schedule, the advertiser must deal with many stations in many markets. In each market the advertiser must select a station or stations. Then, for each station, it is necessary to (1) determine whether the desired time or inventory is available; (2) negotiate for price; (3) place an order; (4) make sure the commercial was played as scheduled, or, if preemptible, learn when it was played; (5) follow up on a make-good if it appeared at a later time; (6) check the bills; and, most important, (7) continually monitor response for potential schedule readjustments. One can readily imagine the complexities that can occur when a direct marketer attempts to promote a product in as many as fifty markets. Fortunately, the increased use of the computer in keeping track of spot transactions has greatly enhanced the ability of the direct marketer to roll out to many markets with much less difficulty than in the past. Many of the advertising agencies that handle direct marketers' promotions, for example, now utilize computers for tracking the progress of a promotion.

PACKAGE FLEXIBILITIES

As we have mentioned, if you purchase preemptible run-of-station or similar packages, you will not have much choice where your commercials will be run. Some run-of-station packages can be 6 A.M. until sign-off. At the same time, you may have to commit to an advertising schedule that can be eight to sixteen weeks in length. There are a few things that you can do, however, to increase the success of these packages.

If you can establish a good relationship with the station manager and have been a good customer in the past, sometimes it is possible to negotiate guaranteed program adjacencies or day parts, even though the package is run-of-station. These guarantees can be beneficial for the station and for you. The station can keep you as a customer who will continue to purchase that station's excess inventory of time. And you are better off because you are getting the time slots you need to produce acceptable results.

There is another bit of flexibility that you can introduce into preemptible package purchases. You can always remove your unproductive promotions, of course, but oftentimes stations will not be happy with you for doing this and will be less inclined to deal with you the next time you want to use their station for a promotion.

There is another solution. Because direct response results have such rapid feedback, usually within a few days, you can determine fairly quickly if your promotion is paying out. Instead of pulling a schedule from a station that is not paying out over your normal testing period, consider replacing the ad that is currently running with a variation of the same commercial or with a commercial that promotes another one of your products. Some direct marketers, in fact, provide stations with one or more alternative ads to be used when the first ad does not produce sufficient response.

PER INQUIRY

Per Inquiry (PI) is an agreement with a television station to broadcast a commercial at no charge or very little charge. In return, the station receives a set commission for every order the advertiser receives. The practice of PI advertising on network and independent stations is very rare today. There are two reasons for this: (1) most stations have little free inventory and need not take a chance with a questionable product or products; and (2) the extra cost of handling the orders from several different product promotions can be time-consuming and difficult to monitor.

The PI form of advertising may become nonexistent as more stations opt for the security of the guaranteed income that spot purchases provide. From the point of view of the marketer, this is both good and bad. For direct marketers with little capital, PI is the ideal way to get off the ground. For very little money the ad can get on the air and begin to pay out with little downside risk. If the marketer can find a PI station, which is difficult, the next hurdle is trying to get on the air. The marketer must be able to convince the station of the profitability of his or her product. The best way to do this is to show the past performance of the product from promotions on other stations or even from other media.

The negative aspect of PI advertising is that if a product is extremely successful, the profits will not be nearly as significant as they would have been had the commercial been run with spot or run-of-station packages. Spot purchases are essentially fixed one-time costs, while PI advertising is variable, relative to the number of orders received.

Station managers not currently offering PI advertising may want to reconsider that option. As direct response marketers become increasingly successful (as reflected in returns), the extra time and expense involved in keeping track of PI response may be more than offset by the revenue generated through PI commissions. In some cases this revenue could be substantial. The extra revenue generated by promotions using the PI system could in fact equal or exceed the revenue derived from the most expensive nonpreemptible spot purchases.

PI opportunities for direct marketers are more prevalent in radio and on cable television stations. Further information about PI can be found in the chapters that discuss the principles of radio and cable television EDM.

COMMERCIAL CONTENT

The EDM commercial is composed of all of the motivational elements that make direct marketing effective in other media. Many direct marketers prefer to use the AIDA formula, or a modification of it, when structuring the commercial message. The acronym AIDA stands for Attention, Interest, Desire, and Action. The EDM commercial is developed to conform to these four elements in the same alphabetical order as the acronym.

Attention

The first part of your commercial should draw attention to your message. If you do not gain the consumer's attention immediately, the rest of your message is essentially lost. You want an opening statement or visual with a sound effect that not only gains attention, but that is also designed to appeal to your target audience. For example, a record offer will begin with a sample of one of the songs from the album. The song immediately defines the audience you are trying to reach and illustrates one of the benefits of receiving the album.

Interest

Now that you have your audience's attention, tell them what your product will do for them. *Time* magazine drives this point home in its EDM ads for subscriptions to its magazine. One of *Time*'s ads shows a man isolated from the outside world whose only source of news and information is *Time* magazine. As he turns the pages of the magazine, the viewer can see and is told about the various features shown in each week's issue, and is also told how he or she can benefit from a subscription.

Desire

Desire is created in any number of ways. It is an attempt to turn the interest you have created into a desire to obtain the advertised product. Most commonly, desire is created by giving your ad a sense of urgency and a reason why the consumer just cannot do without the product. You may, for example, show an actor who represents your target audience enjoying the benefits of using your product.

Action

Present a reason why the consumer should act immediately. The success of your ad hinges on your ability to turn the desire you have created into action. If you do not get the consumer to act within moments after the commercial is over, your probability of getting a response is drastically reduced. And even if the urge to respond has been successfully created within the consumer, that urge may only last for a brief time. Studies have shown, for example, that up to two thirds of the telephone response from a television EDM ad occurs within a few minutes of the airing of the commercial. If lines are jammed and the consumer gets a busy signal, there is a low probability that the consumer will attempt a later callback.

Some common action-producing devices include offering a premium for an immediate order, price discounts, or "two for the price of one" specials. Record offers, for example, often offer sets of two albums for the price of a single album.

The AIDA formula has many variations, but most variations include the four basics of Attention, Interest, Desire, and Action.

CREDIBILITY

Remember that you are asking consumers to purchase an unfamiliar product from an unfamiliar company and from someone they have never seen before, all in the space of 120 seconds or less. Anything that you can do to establish credibility in your ad will help to make your selling job easier. The following suggestions should help you to achieve that goal.

1. Credibility begins with a well-produced ad. Consumers will be less inclined to purchase from you if they perceive your ad to be sloppily produced and cheaply made. The perception of the ad carries over to the perception of the quality of the product.

2. Stress the quality of your product. Point out features and benefits. Offer testimonials from satisfied customers. Most important, show the product in action. Many years of EDM ads for poorly built gadgets and gimmicks have built up an immediate negative or suspicious reaction to many of the products sold through EDM channels. In order to overcome this negative inertia, stressing the quality of your product becomes a necessity.

3. Offer a guarantee. By law, every EDM ad must offer a money-back guarantee. But don't bury your guarantee in small print beneath the telephone number or address. Proudly announce your guarantee and terms. The guarantee shows that you have confidence in your product. It is especially important when you are selling an unfamiliar product. The consumer needs to know that he or she will not be stuck with a worthless product. It removes the *risk* of ordering for the consumer.

4. Probably the most important contributor to the credibility of your ad is the announcer, the actor, or the voice-over that will be used. The announcer can make or break your ad. Long gone are the days of the fast-talking salesman pitching his wares to an unsuspecting public. Honesty and sincerity must come across in your ads, no matter whether it's in the tone of the announcer's voice or in the nonverbal cues given by the actor who is demonstrating your product.

COMMERCIAL LENGTH

There are few rules to follow regarding an appropriate commercial length for your ad. Preliminary testing will usually dictate the most effective length for an EDM ad, but the length may need to be varied, depending upon the market and the ad's objective. The commercial must be long enough to transmit all of the pertinent selling points of the product or service. Generally, the direct-sales commercial is longer than the direct-lead and can be up to 120 seconds or more in length.

There are two main reasons for the extra length of the direct-sale EDM ad. First of all, unlike the direct-lead ad that attempts to get a person to call or write for information, the direct-sale ad is trying to convince the customer to buy the product. More time may be needed to generate that response.

Secondly, most direct-sale ads must present all of the pertinent features and benefits of the product so the consumer has enough information upon which to base a purchasing decision. Some products require more lengthy demonstration than others. For example, gadgets such as vegetable choppers, super knives, and fishing tools fall into this category. Advertisers of record offers rely upon playing several songs from the album, hoping that at least one of the songs will catch the fancy of the consumer and influence the decision to order. *Sports Illustrated* and *Time* magazines often use 90 to 120 seconds to present the scope of their magazines' contents.

Direct-lead EDM ads, especially locally produced and broadcast commercials, are generally not as lengthy as direct sales ads. You are not as concerned about attempting to demonstrate all the various features and benefits of your product, nor are you trying to close the sale in the space of one or two minutes. The close comes later with follow-up contact outside of the television medium.

Local direct marketers, besides sometimes having small budgets, many times find that the less expensive thirty- or sixty-second commercials are their most effective lead producers. One West Coast marketer using direct lead EDM found that his most productive response came from the use of a thirty-second commercial within a program, followed up at the end of the program by a ten-second reminder ad that repeated the telephone number.

Exceptions to the short direct lead EDM commercial are common. Higher-priced items, products with many features and benefits, and many nationally produced direct-lead offers, such as insurance offers, often run longer than sixty seconds. National Home Life Insurance, for example, uses a two-minute commercial to produce leads.

THE ADDRESS AND TELEPHONE NUMBER

Another part of the EDM commercial that adds to length is the need to provide an "800" number or address, as well as the price and other ordering information (cash, COD, credit cards). This time length can be reduced by flashing the "800" number throughout the commercial, alerting the consumer to the fact that ordering information will need to be recorded. The "800" number alone reduces the amount of time needed to record information and also eliminates the confusion caused when the consumer is trying to write down the number and the address before the commercial goes off the air.

You must be sure that you are allotting enough time within your commercial for ordering information. It is absolutely essential that the customer be able to easily record your address or telephone number. Remember, the customer does not necessarily have a pencil and paper readily available. You should repeat the address or phone number at least three times while you are displaying it on the screen. How much time will that take? That depends on whether you are using a telephone number, an address, or both. A combined address and telephone number may take up to thirty seconds to properly communicate to the consumer.

The time you should allot to ordering is relatively fixed, no matter how short or long the commercial. The shorter your commercial, the larger the portion of your commercial that will be dedicated to ordering information.

TRENDS IN COMMERCIAL LENGTH

Average commercial length has been decreasing over the last five years. Today the trend is toward the sixty-second EDM commercial. One of the reasons for the shorter length is that any length over sixty seconds can often be difficult to place, especially in high-demand periods and on network affiliates.

Decreased commercial length does not necessarily mean that a commercial will be less effective. A consumer who has been repeatedly exposed to the same or same type of commercial has more than likely gained a certain familiarity with it and the EDM process. The shorter EDM ad may be all that is needed to spur the consumer to pick up the telephone or to write for the product. You should consider the possibility of shortening your EDM ads. The reduced costs for spots and the increased flexibility in placing shorter spots may enable you to increase response and lower cost per order. Initial testing, however, especially for direct-sale EDM ads, should begin at the traditional 120-second length.

The rapid growth of cable television and the availability of numerous cable channels is opening up new marketing avenues for EDM. Not only are EDM commercials used extensively on these channels, but they also give marketers the opportunity to experiment with longer commercial lengths. Some channels, for example, have home shopping shows composed entirely of EDM-type commercials.

CHOOSING THE ADVERTISING AGENCY

The advertising agency with which you choose to work should be experienced in creating and producing EDM commercials. Agencies with no background in this area will not understand and will neglect to incorporate into your ad all the direct-marketing fundamentals that are so crucial to making an EDM promotion work. Up until a few years ago most of the larger agencies looked down their noses at direct response, considering it something of an ugly stepchild of the more glamorous and prestigious general advertising world. With the increased popularity and success of EDM and direct marketing in recent years, however, most of these agencies have created separate departments or subsidiaries devoted entirely to direct-marketing promotions. Still, most of the major agencies working with EDM are located in Chicago or on the East Coast. There are, however, an increasing number of smaller agencies and production companies located across the country that are gaining experience in working with EDM. One of these agencies may be located near you. There are several sources that can provide you with information about agencies in your area. Your local television station, for example, may be able to suggest an agency appropriate for your needs. Your public library may have a copy of the *Standard Directory of Advertising Agencies,* published by the National Register Publishing Company in Skokie, Illinois. This directory provides a list of all agencies that specialize or have departments in direct response. The main listing section of the directory contains descriptive information about the agencies, including lists of accounts, names and titles of executives, yearly billings, number of employees, and addresses and telephone numbers. Some of these agencies are more experienced than others in EDM promotions. Write to or talk with several of them in your area.

What will the agency do for you? First of all, it will take your product and promotional ideas, and work with you to create your EDM ad. It will develop a script containing the dialogue and the descriptions of desired visual and audio effects. The script will then be appliqued to a storyboard, essentially a frame-by-frame description of the commercial. Each frame will contain a drawing illustrating the visual activity that is intended for that particular point in the commercial. Beneath the picture are the spoken words that will be used for that part of the commercial, as well as words describing any special visual or audio effects that will be used.

The script and storyboard, once they have been approved, become the basis for your commercial and are translated by the producer and the director into the finished commercial.

EDM COSTS

How much does it cost to produce, test, and roll out an EDM promotion? Historically, budgets for direct-response promotions have been significantly less than budgets allocated for general advertising promotions. Most direct marketers spent as little as possible for commercial production. As a result, the commercials, although effective, were sloppily produced and shoddy looking. Up until a few years ago it was possible to produce and test an EDM promotion for as little as $5,000 to $10,000. Low costs such as these are now the exception, but costs are still well below those of most general advertising campaigns.

Production and testing costs now run anywhere from $10,000 to $50,000 or more, depending on the size and quality of the promotion. Several factors will determine how much you will need to spend. Let's discuss each of the major cost and quality variables you will need to consider.

Testing Costs

Will your promotion be local or national in scope? If you intend to roll out your promotion on a national scale, for example, your production and testing costs will need to be much greater than a local promotion. Testing costs alone may be as much as $30,000 for spot purchases, depending on the number of markets and spots you will use, although it is possible to test for much less than this.

Eventual roll-outs can amount to up to a million dollars or more for well-financed national campaigns. Your roll-out budget (your anticipated cash flow needs) can be determined by multiplying your estimated sales volume times your maximum acceptable cost per order.

The costs you will incur for testing will more than likely not be sunk costs. That is, because each commercial generates revenue, most, if not all, of your testing costs should be recovered. These revenues can then be reapplied to the resources allocated for the roll-out.

Production Costs

Station versus Local Producer: Most local television stations have the facilities to produce your ad. You will find in most cases that the costs of using your local television station will be much less than those of utilizing the services of an independent producer. The station can turn out a commercial for you quickly, efficiently, and inexpensively. Unfortunately, the quality of the commercial may not be as good as the commercial produced by the independent producer. If your commercial will be aired locally or regionally, the commercial produced by your local television station may be acceptable for your needs. But if you intend to roll out nationally with your ad, you should consider enlisting the services of an independent producer.

Production Estimates: If you decide to use an independent producer, it is wise to obtain estimates of production costs from several of them. You will be surprised how much costs can vary from producer to producer for the same commercial, sometimes as much as 100 percent. There are usually good reasons for these cost differences. The experience and reputation of the producer, the approach to shooting the commercial, and the talent level of cast and crew all play a part in the total cost of the estimate.

Before choosing a producer, make sure you see some of his or her past work to get an idea of past performance. It is especially important to determine if that work was done at a cost comparable to your contemplated budget.

The least expensively bid production may provide you with an acceptable level of quality. In most cases, however, you will find that the old adage "you get what you pay for" is essentially true. A low-cost production will usually look like a low-cost production.

Cost-Plus or Completion Bids? Bidding by producers can be in two forms: cost-plus or completion bid. A cost-plus bid is essentially an open-ended estimate of the cost of producing the commercial. Costs of additional takes or production costs above the original estimate become a part of the total cost that you must pay. Although the cost-plus bid is flexible in terms of the additional freedom it gives the director during shooting, the costs can amount to much more than originally estimated.

The completion bid is a set estimate of the costs required to complete the commercial. Any charges or additional costs incurred during production must be absorbed by the producer. The completion bid is probably the better alternative for you. If you choose a producer with high standards, he or she will see that your commercial is done right, even though that may cost the producer a bit more than the original estimate.

Film or Videotape? An important production consideration is choosing between the use of film or videotape to record your commercial. Each of the mediums has its advantages and disadvantages, and most agencies and producers have a favorite, but the main criterion that should influence your decision to use film or tape is the visual image you are trying to achieve.

Film has long been a favorite medium for the general advertiser. Most of the national network spots you see on television are filmed rather than videotaped. One of the main reasons general advertisers prefer film is because of its grainy rich texture. This texture gives the commercial a soft, expensive look.

Videotape, on the other hand, is the favorite medium of the direct response marketer. Videotape images are sharper, harsher, cleaner, and give the impression of being more alive or real than film. This cleaner, sharper image has been found to create a feeling of urgency or immediacy in the consumer's mind, a feeling that contributes to the ability of the marketer to motivate the consumer to respond.

Unlike film, which needs to be sent out for processing before editing can occur, videotape is instantaneous. Scenes can be examined as soon as they are shot, and immediate retakes can be shot if necessary. In addition, the technology associated with videotape has improved dramatically in the last few years. Various special effects are available that are now much easier to incorporate into the commercial. Editing capabilities are also improving, especially with the introduction of the computer into the editing process.

There are still situations where film may be appropriate. Support EDM commercials, for example, are produced by agencies that have traditionally filmed their advertisements. These agencies are more comfortable with and prejudiced toward the use of film in their commercials.

The content of your direct-sale or direct-lead ad may dictate the use of film rather than tape. If the product you are trying to promote is expensive, for example, and you believe that the audience you are

40

trying to reach would respond more favorably to the filmed visual image of that product, then film may be more appropriate.

If you use the services of a local television station to produce your commercial, it will more than likely recommend videotape. This is because most stations are better equipped for videotape than film.

It is important that you utilize the services of producers and directors experienced in the medium you choose. Videotape, if used incorrectly, can make your commercial look cheap and shoddy. Poor lighting, incorrect camera angles, and so forth can have a negative influence on the eventual visual quality of the finished product.

TESTING AND ANALYSIS OF RESULTS

The real value of direct-response advertising is its measurability, its ability to tell us within a relatively short period of time the effectiveness of our promotion, whether it be in a test phase or in the middle of a roll-out. The measurement tools inherent in EDM commercials let us closely monitor each commercial or station's performance and, based on results, let us readjust our scheduling to take advantage of the most productive areas of a market or a station.

Testing strategy is dependent on the type of promotion you intend to run. If there is a possibility of a national roll-out, it is to your advantage to test in several markets across the nation rather than in just a few local markets. You may be surprised at the variations in returns from market to market. A promotion that may have been rejected for lack of response in one market may be a complete success in another.

Some products seem to sell better than others in some parts of the country. Sales of records are a good example. Tastes can vary across the country. A country-and-western album that may sell well in the Southwest may produce only marginal returns in other parts of the country.

Appeals can make a difference, too. Testing variations of your offer is important in determining the best kinds of spots to use for your roll-out.

Use the Best Markets

Just as you would start testing with your best list in a direct-mail or telephone campaign, it is advisable to first use those stations or markets you have found to be most productive in past promotions. The theory here is that if the best doesn't pull enough response for you, then other normally less productive markets will not perform any better.

Some EDM Math

The mathematical aspects of testing for direct response are not particularly complex. The basic measurement criteria in both testing and roll-out are cost per sale (order) in a direct sale EDM promotion, and cost per lead or cost per conversion in a direct lead EDM promotion. A simple cost per order calculation might be as follows:

Market 1	Cost	Orders	CPO	Acceptable CPO
Station A	$5,000	550	$9	$6
Station B	$2,000	250	$8	
Station C	$3,000	575	$5	

This example shows that in this particular analysis, Station C is clearly producing acceptable results, compared with the other two stations.

Many advertisers will stop their analysis at this gross cost-per-total-sale point and not stop to consider the viability of individual time purchases. Just because a total time purchase does not produce an acceptable cost per order does not mean that a particular promotion is a failure. A twenty-spot run-of-station purchase, for example, may not pay out overall, but there may have been one, two, or several spots that did extremely well.

STATION B

Spots	Time	Cost/Spot	Total Cost		Orders		CPO
3	Morning	$100	$300		30		$10
2	Daytime	$100	$200		10		$20
2	Early Evening	$200	$400		40		$10
1	Prime Time	$600	$600		45		$13
10	Late Night	$50	$500		125		$4
	Total		$2,000	÷	250	=	$ 8

Now we can see that on Station B, those spot purchases made on the late night time segment produced a CPO of $4, well below the maximum allowable CPO of $6. You can now go back to Station B and maximize your returns by readjusting your spot purchases to include only late night spots.

You aren't quite through with your analysis yet. Most promotions have a certain percentage of products that are returned by customers. If you are selling products COD, for example, you can expect that customer refusals to pay might be high. Returns on CODs have been known to run as high as 25 to 30 percent. If you have a product that is breakable, hard to put together, or that may have a probability of high returns for whatever reason, you must factor potential and actual returns into your projections and actual response rates; for example:

	Cost	Orders	CPO	Returns	Net	CPO	Max CPO
Station D	$3,000	600	$5	100	500	$6	$5

High returns, in this instance, are causing you to exceed your maximum acceptable CPO of $5. If you cannot correct the high return situation, perhaps by increasing the quality of your product, or by switching to credit cards or asking for cash up front, then you will be forced to withdraw this particular promotion.

Telephone and Address for Testing

During the testing period it is advisable to use only the telephone for response. The telephone will provide you with daily and even hourly information as to the effectiveness of your ads. Responses from the address, on the other hand, may require much more time to collect and analyze. The telephone provides you with more flexibility in adjusting schedules to minimize the impact of poor returns in sluggish markets and maximize returns in stronger markets. The telephone, in fact, is now used in a majority of EDM testing situations.

In some cases, however, the address can pull just as well as the telephone. You may want to test to see whether the telephone or the address is the more productive for you. You can do this on a CPO basis by simply dividing the cost of your spots by the number of telephone responses and address responses. Then compare the CPO that each produces.

Be sure to key your address or telephone number so you can keep track of where responses are coming from. You may want to change your telephone number, for example, for each market or station. You can also track response by asking your customers for station and program information when they call in their orders.

Test Spots

Knowing when and where a spot will air will help you to more accurately measure response during the testing phase. For this reason, you may want to purchase nonpreemptible spots rather than run-of-station packages. Even if you do not purchase spots with particular program adjacencies, you should ensure that your spots will air within certain parts of the program day. Rates for spots purchased in this manner will be less than guaranteed program adjacencies, but will still give you a fairly accurate measurement from which to project your roll-out.

Don't give up on your test markets too early. Results may take two or three weeks to build as customers become familiar with your commercial. But after this time, when results begin to taper off, response is not likely to build again, and you should pull the ad as soon as your CPO rises above an acceptable level.

The Application of Split-Run Testing to Television EDM

One advantage of direct-response media such as magazines, newspapers, or direct mail is that they lend themselves to fairly accurate testing techniques. One of these techniques is called the split-run test. The split-run test is a technique used to determine the effectiveness of two or more simultaneously run advertisements. Some newspapers, for example, are equipped to allow advertisers to split-run their advertisements. The newspaper prints these advertisements $(A + B)$ so that one issue contains Ad A and every other issue contains Ad B. The newspaper is distributed normally, except that every other issue sold contains Ad A. With this type of distribution, a marketer can test the effectiveness of Ad A over Ad B and know that his or her results will be representative and reasonably unbiased. Each ad, of course, would have been separately keyed so that response could be accurately assigned to each ad.

Although it may be difficult to approximate publication testing conditions, direct-response television marketers can use variations of the split-run test to determine differences between appeals.

John Caples, one of the deans of advertising and direct marketing and author of the popular book *Tested Advertising Methods*, suggests that the split-run test is transferable to the electronic media.

There is of course no way that the television audience can be split in half so that one half of the sets are exposed to Ad A while the other half are exposed to Ad B. But we can come close to approximating this split.

A marketer may be considering two different commercials, Ad A, and Ad B. Each ad contains a different appeal for a product. Perhaps Ad A stresses price more than quality, and Ad B stresses quality more than price. Before an advertising campaign can begin, the marketer must know which ad will be most response-effective. And because time is money, it is preferable to obtain results as quickly as possible.

In order to get an accurate, relatively unbiased comparison of the effectiveness of the two ads, a procedure must be developed to eliminate or control as many extraneous variables as possible. Caples suggests the following technique to help eliminate some of these variables. It is based on the mechanics of the split-run test.

Commercials A and B will run alternately every other day for two weeks. The schedule would look something like this:

First Week	Ad	Second Week	Ad
Monday	A	Monday	B
Tuesday	B	Tuesday	A
Wednesday	A	Wednesday	B
Thursday	B	Thursday	A
Friday	A	Friday	B

The commercials are run at the same time every day. Keeping the time of day constant helps to keep audience characteristics constant, assuming programming does not vary. The effect of alternating commercials every other day for two weeks allows both commercials equal exposure every day of the week. This alternating of days for two weeks parallels somewhat the concept of split-run testing. Although the two commercials are not run on the same day, they do receive same day exposure one week apart. Commercial B, for example, although not run on Monday of the first week, will be run on Monday of the second week; Commercial B on Tuesday of the first week would be replaced by Ad A on Tuesday of the second week, and so on.

Each commercial should be keyed so that a record of response from each can be kept. If both commercials contained "800" telephone numbers and addresses, for example, then a different telephone number and address should be assigned to each ad.

Depending on time constraints, it may be advisable to use an "800" number only. Response from the mail may take much longer and lengthen the amount of time required to ascertain commercial productivity. The "800" number allows the marketer to record heaviest response days, since most telephone response occurs on the same day that the ad is run. With mail response, the marketer would have little idea which day of the week or which week the response-generating ad was run. The differential between the two commercials may be so significant during the first few days that the second week may not be necessary. An "800" number only would allow this determination to be made and help to lower testing expenses.

This method compensates for the effects of certain days of the week having the heaviest viewing audiences and responses, because both commercials are given equal exposure on these days.

It is possible that the results of advertising your commercials in one market will result in a "contamination" effect. That is, the consumer who responds to Ad A may have been partially influenced by exposure to Ad B. Probably the only way to reduce this bias would be to test these commercials in two homogeneous but separate geographical or market areas. However, you may have difficulty maintaining audience homogeneity by advertising in separate markets. It may be difficult (and more expensive) for you to advertise in similar markets; the task of coordinating the timing of spots, the locating of similar programming, and the ability to obtain spots within those programs may be difficult to accomplish. The possible small differential in bias reduction between a split-run test in one market as compared with a separate market test might indicate that a split-run test in just one market would be accurate enough to assess the viability of one product appeal over another.

Television testing of this type cannot be as precise as split-run testing in other direct-response media. This procedure, however, could eliminate many of the variables that would tend to bias results.

Testing Products for Other
Direct Response Media

One of the major drawbacks in the development of successful promotional packages for direct response marketing is that most of the direct-response media require a considerable amount of lead time and expense before an assessment can be made to determine their effectiveness. For example, a direct-mail campaign necessitates heavy front-end expenses for printing and mailing costs, with little assurance that the first few mailings will indicate sufficient response to at least recoup these expenses. In addition, a considerable amount of time will have transpired before results can be measured and projected. In other direct-response media, such as magazine space ads, lead times of two to three months are not uncommon. Results of these ads may not be in until several weeks after that.

An area of direct-response advertising that could have important application is that of testing products and promotions that will be used within another direct-response medium. Television testing has several distinct advantages over initial testing through the direct-response medium that will eventually be used. Television testing would allow a direct marketer to put together a promotional package, and, within a very short time, have a good idea of its probability for success.

The major shortcoming of this testing approach is that the testing medium is not the actual medium to be used. Some aspects of the promotion may not be transferable to another direct-response medium. For example, a product that requires demonstration to understand its functions may not be sold as easily through direct mail. A marketer can compensate for the lack of personal demonstration with lengthy copy and illustrations to ensure that the consumer understands the operation of the product. Some of the impulse and excitement that television provides, however, will still be lacking.

46

The important point, though, is that a direct-response marketer can use television EDM to get a reasonable approximation of success in other direct-response media, and can determine this with less lead time and quicker response time than other media require. In addition, the marketer may find that a television test of a promotion is so successful that the television medium can also or even exclusively be utilized for the eventual full campaign.

EDM IN OTHER COUNTRIES

Television EDM is not necessarily limited to the United States. Other countries are now beginning to apply direct-marketing techniques to the television medium. Marketers in Canada and the United Kingdom, for example, use television EDM. There are some differences, however, that must be considered before attempting to enter these markets. Television EDM is a relatively new phenomenon in these and other countries. Television viewers are not as conditioned to these broadcasts as the American consumer. For example, "800" numbers, which are effective in the United States, do not work as well in Canada. One reason for this is that Canadians are not as accustomed to using these numbers as are Americans.

Many of the mechanics of television EDM are transferable to other countries, but, depending on the country, knowledge of the differences is important if the direct marketers want to increase probabilities for success.

Summary of Important Points

Television EDM is ideal for virtually any product or service promotion.

Television has the potential to outperform similar promotions in other media.

The cost of television time to produce acceptable, profitable results need not be expensive; low-cost time on lower-rated programs may increase response levels.

Quality commercial production is an important contributor to response.

Your commercial should contain elements to gain attention, generate interest, create desire, and spur the customer to action.

Make your commercial message believable.

Commercial length is dependent upon your product, your resources, ordering instructions, and the availability of time.

Carefully select your advertising agency or producer.

It is important to test your promotions before roll-out.

Measuring response (testing) is necessary to keep close tabs on results. You should test beyond the simple CPO per station, and test for response within specific time segments. Remember to measure returns.

The split-run test can help you to quickly test for the best commercial appeal.

You can use EDM to test a promotion that will be rolled out in another medium.

4

SUPPORT EDM

Support EDM is the use of television (or radio, or the telephone) as a secondary medium to support a direct-marketing effort within another direct response medium such as newspapers, magazines, or direct mail. Support advertising differs from direct-lead and direct-sales EDM in that support EDM is designed to call attention to another primary medium that carries the direct response offer. Because the intent of support EDM is to draw attention to another medium, the mechanics of the implementation of support EDM are not the same as those utilized in direct-sale and direct-lead EDM.

The concept of support advertising has been with us for many years. We've mentioned that more than twenty-five years ago, *Reader's Digest* launched a radio campaign urging listeners to look in their mailboxes for a subscription offer. Today the largest users of support EDM include insurance companies, book and magazine publishers, and record companies. Publisher's Clearing House, for example, advertises its sweepstakes-oriented direct-mail campaign extensively on television. Columbia Records and Tapes, Time-Life, and National Home Life Insurance are also examples of companies that use television support.

There are several reasons why a direct marketer might wish to use a support medium rather than concentrate expenditures and effort in the primary medium: (1) Perception of an advertising message can be enhanced with exposure from more than one medium. (2) The audio and visual stimulus provided by television can be a positive factor in understanding or interpreting the advertising message. (3) The added exposure of the television message can increase awareness, and, if properly promoted, can overcome skepticism and increase believability. (Publisher's Clearing House, for example, overcame the problems of skepticism and believability surrounding their sweepstakes promotions. It was found that most consumers felt that they did not have a chance to win any of the prizes and therefore did not respond to the promotions. The solution to this problem was to utilize television to show actual winners and their prizes.) (4) Marketers are finding that, frequently, the more media that are utilized in a given market, the greater the response.

Response Rates

The impact of television support to returns can be significant. For example, if a print campaign is run without television support, an advertiser might expect to receive, say, 10,000 orders. By adding television at an X amount of dollars, perhaps 15,000 orders might be received. If these extra 5,000 orders can be obtained at or near the same cost per order as the original 10,000 orders, then this increase can represent a significant value to the marketer.

What kind of response, then, can a direct marketer expect from a television-supported campaign? Some advertisers have reported an increase of 50 percent or more, using 5 to 10 percent of the total advertising budget. One researcher reported that a television-supported preprint campaign resulted in a 41-percent reduction in cost per response, and an increase in total response of 95 percent.

Reports like these are good news to direct marketers searching for ways to enhance the effectiveness of their marketing campaigns. Rising costs, particularly in direct-response media other than television, make it increasingly important that new techniques are developed to boost response and at the same time lower or maintain cost per order. Support EDM is allowing marketers to do just that.

Penetration Levels

Because of the relative newness of support advertising, most marketers are still uncertain exactly how much support should be given to the primary medium. Marketer and researcher estimates have ranged from 5 percent of budget to 100 percent of the total advertising dollar investment in the primary medium for additional allocation in television support. One generally accepted principle, however, is that before a support campaign can be launched, it must be ascertained the extent to which the primary medium is penetrating the existing market. A minimum of 25 percent penetration into the primary medium is usually considered to be the level below which television support can become too costly.

ADVERTISING PRINCIPLES

Unlike direct-sale and direct-lead EDM, which are concerned with low-cost spot buys on programs with low attentiveness levels, support EDM spot purchases follow the rules of general consumer advertising. Support EDM attempts to reach as many targeted consumers in the primary medium as possible, as many times as possible, and in a manner as cost-effective as possible, within the constraints of the advertising budget.

Reach, frequency, and rating points, for example, are important considerations for a support purchase. Reach is the number of unduplicated households that are exposed to an advertising message. Frequency refers to the number of times an individual or household is exposed to a medium within a given time period. A commercial must be run at least six times to be regarded as representing frequency.

Each time period of the television day also has a maximum reach potential. For example, the maximum reach potential of men 18–49 years old during the early evening in a particular market may be 65 percent. No matter how many times a spot is run, reach will not exceed the maximum reach potential of 65 percent.

Reach and frequency considerations may also vary by product and market.

A rating point measures reach and frequency. One rating point is the equivalent of 1 percent penetration of the households in a market. Television programs are expressed in terms of gross rating points (GRPs). GRPs are determined by the rating points a program receives (reach), multiplied by the number of times a commercial is run on that program (frequency). For example, if a commercial runs on a program that has a rating of 5 once a week for six weeks, the gross rating points will be 30. The relationship of reach and frequency to gross rating points can be expressed in the following way:

$$R \times F = GRP \qquad F = Frequency$$
$$R = Reach$$

$$GRP/R = F$$

$$GRP/F = R$$

(For example, if an advertiser wanted to purchase 180 GRPs during a time period that had a reach of 55 percent or 55 rating points: GRP/F = 180/55 = a frequency of 3.3.)

The gross rating point process provides a common base for determining support levels regardless of market size. For example, 180 gross rating points in Spokane, which has 295,700 television homes, will give an advertiser the same reach and frequency as Chicago, which has 2,875,300 television homes. Cost per rating point, however, varies from market to market, because it is dependent on supply and demand.

Because the concept of support television advertising and the application of gross rating point purchasing to the support medium is essentially in its infancy, the levels of GRP purchases in a market area frequently are arbitrary decisions based upon limited experience. Before an extensive campaign can be rolled out, an advertiser must also test to determine minimum primary medium penetration. Depending upon the marketer, this testing may involve different forms of analysis and degrees of sophistication. Nearly always, however, consideration is given to reach, frequency, and GRPs.

SUPPORT ANALYSIS TECHNIQUES

Support Efficiency Ratio

One of the more sophisticated support analysis techniques used today was developed by the advertising agency of Wunderman, Ricotta, and Kline, and is discussed by Jerome S. Lieb in an article in *Direct Marketing* called "Penetrating Television Market Using Direct Marketing Skills." The technique is called the Support Efficiency Ratio. The concept was developed as a result of attempts to discover ways to evaluate markets for newspaper preprints that were to be supported by television advertising. Through an analysis of newspaper circulations in designated market areas, the advertiser is able to determine the extent to which newspaper circulation falls within the primary signal reach of each television station in the market. The designated market area (DMA) is an A. C. Nielson Company determination of the audience saturation levels of specific television stations on a county-by-county basis. The process of calculating this penetration is made easier in market areas that have only one newspaper. In a DMA such as Seattle, for example, which has several major newspapers, it is also necessary to determine the number of unduplicated households in order to find the net unduplicated households in the market. These data can then be used to ascertain whether or not newspaper penetration is sufficient to warrant television support.

52

These data in themselves are not really sufficient to allow an advertiser to make decisions regarding support levels and costs. Not only are support levels in themselves sometimes arbitrary decisions; television costs can vary from market to market as well as within various parts of the program day.

The product being promoted in the primary medium will determine the target audience you intend to reach with television. This means that your spot purchases need to be within those programs or day parts where your target audience will most likely be watching. For example, female-oriented products require heavier use of daytime spots than male-oriented products.

After a budget has been chosen (that is, the GRPs have been decided upon), the amount that will be spent within each day part is estimated. Each budget for a market area can then be compared in the form of a ratio to market circulation within a designated market area (cost/circulation), and a cost per thousand unduplicated household reach figure can be derived. For example, if the newspaper circulation (unduplicated) in the DMA of Seattle is 500,000 and the television support budget is $5,000, the cost per thousand would be $10.

Determining Lift

Let's work through a slightly different kind of analysis:

Assumptions: You are putting together a direct-mail campaign and want to determine how much "lift" (additional response) will be needed to recoup expenses allocated to television support in a selected DMA.

- Direct mailing: 500,000 pieces
- Cost: $175,000
- Cost per thousand (CPM): $350
- Television support: You want to buy enough GRPs to provide 75 percent reach.
- Cost: $10,000
- Total households in DMA: 1,000,000
- Total households using television in DMA: 90 percent, or 900,000.
- Number of television households in DMA receiving your mailing: 90 percent × 500,000 = 450,000.
- Percent of television homes receiving your mailing: 450/900 = 50 percent.
- Number of households seeing your television ad and receiving a direct mailing: (900) (0.75) (0.50) = 338,000.
- CPM to reach television households that received your direct mailing: $10,000/338 = $30.
- Total CPM direct mail and support: $350 + $30 = $380.
- Lift required: 30/350 = 9 percent.

Looking at cost in terms of lift can be beneficial. For example, if the cost per thousand for your primary medium were significantly lower and your support CPM remained the same, the required percentage of lift would be correspondingly higher, possibly higher than a level that you feel your support advertising can produce.

It should be pointed out that there is quite a bit of subjectivity in these and all support analysis techniques. Many of the variables used for analysis are arbitrary decisions based upon limited experience with a particular product or promotion, or a lack of knowledge about the potential impact of changing levels of support. The amount of GRPs to purchase for a given product, for example, is up to the advertiser. Choices of where and when to purchase spots may vary, depending on the advertiser's profile of customer characteristics. But although support analysis techniques have their drawbacks, they nevertheless provide the marketer with a tool with which to work. These techniques are predictive models that have been shown to be successful in direct marketing decision-making situations. They allow the marketer to estimate the potential reach of the support advertising and allow the marketer to see if cost estimates are in an agreeable range. In addition, the CPM ratio is used in other media and can be compared to costs of promotions in other media.

The intent of these and other measurement techniques is to help marketers make reasonable decisions before and during testing, giving them the tools not only to estimate and eliminate obviously impractical campaigns, but to enhance the probabilities for successful rollouts as well.

TESTING RESPONSE DIFFERENTIALS

In order to determine the effectiveness of a *supported* versus a *non-supported* campaign, the marketer must test to determine whether support is a worthwhile investment of resources. This testing can take several forms but in general involves the isolation of test markets, some of which have had television support and some of which have not. For example, you may decide to run a space campaign with an insert in a magazine that has an extensive national distribution. You can then select several markets and use television support in those markets. By keying each market separately on your insert, you can then establish a correlation between the test markets and the rest that have no support.

When the ad is run a second time, do not provide television support to the test markets. You can then compare your test markets with the previously supported markets and to the rest of the nonsupported markets to determine the difference that support advertising makes.

Because you know your costs, those differences should not be too difficult to estimate.

THE TRANSFER DEVICE

The testing of supported advertising has in the past been a complex procedure, usually requiring large expenditures of money and time. Results were not truly precise but more of an estimate. A relatively simple innovation for accurately measuring the results of television support has only recently been applied within the support ads of such corporations as Time-Life, Inc. and Columbia Records and Tapes. The innovation is called a transfer device, and its discovery is generally attributed to the advertising agency of Wunderman, Ricotta, and Kline.

The transfer device works as follows: The consumer is informed during the support broadcast that his or her mail (or newspaper, or magazine) includes a product offering from that company. The consumer is then told that within this print offer is a "secret" box that is known only to those individuals who are watching the television advertisement. This "secret" box is a blank space that can be filled in by the consumer with a word or number. In return, the consumer will receive a free gift along with the product order. Columbia Records and Tapes, for example, tells the consumer than an extra free record or tape can be ordered by writing the identification number of the desired record or tape in this space. Time-Life uses this space to offer a free book or promotion-related gift such as a poster. A company that advertises the "Bullworker" exercise machine offers a free medallion if the consumer places a check mark in the "secret" box.

The transfer device can help the marketer in two ways: It is a measurement device and it is a response motivator.

Response to these free offers can be measured more accurately than support advertising that only reminds the consumer of the primary medium offer. The advertiser can easily count the responses resulting from "secret" box support ads, whereas increased response from "reminder" support ads can only be estimated. Calculations of the support effectiveness of "secret" ads are based upon more concrete data and allow for more confidence in projections. The relationships between past nonsupported primary medium advertising and present support advertising within the same or similar markets must still be estimated, however. If this relationship is not considered, the difficulty still remains in estimating how many consumers would have ordered a product without support. That is, a simple count may not be an exact estimater of support effectiveness.

It has been found that the desire created by the transfer device provides an impetus somewhat stronger than normal reminder support advertising, thereby creating a greater support impact on the primary medium.

COMMERCIAL LENGTH AND CONTENT

Generally, a support commercial is not as long as a traditional television EDM commercial. Support commercials as short as ten seconds have been used effectively to support the primary medium. Most support commercials, however, are thirty to sixty seconds in length. One detail that allows the marketer to reduce the length of the commercial is that there is no need to provide ordering information, which normally takes fifteen to thirty seconds of a direct-lead or -sale EDM commercial. Instead, the support commercial concentrates on drawing attention to and generating excitement for the offer in the primary medium. In addition to dramatizing the offer, the ad should emphasize the medium where and when the offer will appear (Sunday paper, next week's *Newsweek*, and so on), what the offer looks like (perhaps the actor will hold up the newspaper insert, or show the front of the magazine), and how to order (in the case of a record offer, for example, the television ad may show a consumer choosing records and then mailing the order). One item that may lengthen the commercial is the inclusion of the transfer device. It may take fifteen or twenty seconds for the actor to show the consumer what needs to be done in order to receive a free gift (circle secret number, put an "x" in box, and so on).

TIMING AND COORDINATION
OF SUPPORT CAMPAIGNS

Unlike direct-lead and direct-sale EDM campaigns, which are not dependent upon another medium for a roll-out, support EDM campaigns need to be closely coordinated with the dates of direct mailings, inserts, or space ads. For this reason, spots purchased to support the primary medium must air at a specified time and date. Ad costs, therefore, will be higher, because spots must be nonpreemptible (for the most part) rather than typical run-of-station EDM spots. Not only are costs higher, but also, because the support schedule is dependent upon the primary medium advertising schedule, a mix-up in dates or advertising delays in the primary medium can seriously reduce the effectiveness of the support medium. For this reason, it is important to ensure that the primary medium advertising does not differ from the proposed schedule. If it does, you will need to readjust your support schedule to correlate with those differences.

EXPANSION BEYOND NORMAL SEASONAL CONSTRAINTS

Most direct marketers find that their best responses to direct mailings, space ads, newspaper preprints, and so on, occur during certain months of the year. At other times of the year, response rates may not be significant enough to attempt a direct-marketing promotional campaign, even though the promoted product may not be particularly seasonal in nature. The marketer's ability to grow is therefore severely restricted by the limiting factor of marginal returns in off months. In a case such as this, support EDM may prove to be effective in increasing overall response. The summertime, for example, is normally a poor time of the year for direct mailings. Response is generally much lower during this time, and many marketers find they cannot get adequate returns. Mailing costs remain high and returns are lower; therefore cost per order may exceed acceptable parameters.

Support EDM may be the answer to increasing marginal returns during these time periods. The added lift provided by support advertising could increase returns to a satisfactory level and still maintain or even reduce cost per order. The net result is the ability of the direct marketer to shake seasonal constraints and expand the business into a year-round operation.

APPLICATION OF SUPPORT EDM TO OTHER PRODUCTS

At the present time there are a limited number of products that utilize support advertising. Magazines, books, and records are virtually the only products being promoted in this manner, and these by only a few companies. Certainly other product promotions using support EDM should be attempted. If a product promotion can meet the criterion of minimum penetration levels into the market within the primary medium, it may be worthwhile to attempt some support in limited markets to determine its effectiveness. As more accurate testing procedures are developed, and as the lifts that can be gained from support EDM become documented, it is likely that an increasing number of marketers will begin to adopt support EDM as a promotional vehicle.

Summary of Important Points

Support EDM can effectively enhance returns in the primary medium.

Penetration levels in the primary medium should exceed 25 percent.

Support EDM follows the rules of general advertising. Reach, frequency, and rating points are all considered in planning the promotion.

The transfer device is an accurate response measurement tool and is used to motivate additional response.

Support EDM can enhance response to many other product and service promotions not currently using the technique.

5

RADIO EDM

Radio is as much a part of our lives as television and the telephone. Radio is the voice that the public relies upon for entertainment, news, and information. Today more than 500 million radio sets are in use in 80 million homes. That's 99 percent of all the homes in the United States, and an average of more than six sets per home! And 99 percent of all cars in the United States are equipped with radios as well.

Radio is an excellent medium for direct-marketing promotions. In fact, radio EDM is more prevalent than most direct marketers realize. According to Dr. Julian L. Simon, professor of economics and marketing at the University of Illinois, Urbana, and the author of the book *How to Start and Operate a Mail Order Business*, radio carries more direct-response advertising than television. Statistics on radio EDM are scarce, but there are several factors that seem to support this statement, especially if one is talking about the number of EDM advertisements that are broadcast on radio. There are more than 8,700 radio stations in the United States, roughly divided between AM and FM. The proportion of EDM ads to regular ads is roughly equivalent in radio and TV. Compared with the number of television stations in operation (1008), radio broadcasts more than eight times as many EDM ads than does television.

Radio should not be overlooked as a direct-marketing medium. Oftentimes direct marketers ignore radio and opt instead for the glamour of television. This is unfortunate because radio has much to offer to the direct marketer. In fact, radio should be one of the first mediums, if not *the* first medium, to be considered when planning a direct-response promotion. There are several reasons for this.

Radio Is a Personal Medium. Radio listeners are very loyal. Studies show that listeners prefer to listen to their favorite stations rather than to specific programs. Television viewers, on the other hand, couldn't care less about what station they are turned to; they turn to a television station to watch a specific program. Once you understand the demographics of your listeners in radio, the positioning of your EDM ads becomes less of a concern than when placing an EDM ad on television, because your radio audience makeup is station-specific rather than program-specific.

Radio Is a Selective, Segmentable Medium. Most radio stations today have narrow program formats. These formats can be quite diverse, ranging from all news or talk show formats to all classical music. In fact, *Standard Rates and Data* for radio lists well over 200 different program formats.

Excellent demographic information is also available that will help you to understand the kind of audience that listens to these formats. For example, a rock music station will attract teenage listeners, a classical music station will attract older listeners, and so on.

Both the narrow program formatting and readily available demographic information allow the direct marketer to be very specific in targeting his or her promotion to the right audience. This ability to target the right audience, when combined with the right product and promotion, greatly increases the chances that your EDM promotion will be successful. You will be making more effective use of your resources because you will be able to generate a higher volume of orders for the audience you reach as well as a lower cost per order than you might be able to achieve elsewhere.

Radio Is Inexpensive. Compared with other direct-marketing mediums, radio can be much less expensive. Direct-mail costs, for example, can be as high as $300 per thousand or more. The cost of time on radio, however, averages less than $2 per thousand. But where the most significant savings can occur is in the area of production. If, for example, you write the script for your ad and mail it in to the station to be read live by the announcer, production costs can be $0. Even a studio-produced tape may cost less than $200.

Radio Is Flexible. A radio EDM promotion can be put together and tested in a relatively short period of time, and a marketer can be in and out of a market much faster in radio than in almost any other medium. Lead times needed to get a promotion on the air are usually days or even weeks less than television, and can be months less than a direct-mail or magazine promotion. In addition, if the telephone is used to measure response, results can be obtained almost immediately.

Changes in a promotion can be made fairly easily and inexpensively, in many cases literally overnight. Scripts can be rewritten, tapes can be rerecorded, prices changed, or terms revised without a significant loss of time or money. Responses to changes in promotions can be measured, and a solid, finished package can be worked out in short order before promotions in other media have even begun. As a result, your resources are not tied up for long periods of time, and if a test proves successful, you can quickly reallocate those resources for a roll-out.

Radio Is Transferable to Other Media. Because of radio's segmentability and definable demographics, test results obtained in radio can frequently approximate the results that might be achieved in other direct marketing mediums. These results can be projected to other media, taking into account the changes necessary to create the same appeal in the other media (for example, visual additions for television or additional descriptive copy for direct mail). In the same respect, a direct-response promotion that is successful in another medium can be successful in radio, unless the product or service needs to be seen or is too complex to describe within radio's audio limitations. Even in those cases, a promotion that may have been a direct-sale or one-step process in another medium could be converted into a direct-lead or two-step process in radio.

There is some disagreement among marketers whether radio should be used as the initial test medium for a promotion. Some marketers contend that radio does not give a true picture of results that could be achieved in another medium. They contend that if a promotion fails in radio, that does not necessarily mean that it won't be successful on television, for example, and that a true test of a promotion should be within the eventual medium that will be used. This author does not disagree that radio is an imprecise tool for measuring potential responsiveness in other media, but there may be good reason to make the initial EDM test in radio. Various appeals, prices, times, and so on can be tried. Knowledge can be gained about the audience that will respond to your promotion, and the promotion can be redirected to key in on that audience.

Another important reason for using radio first is cost. An EDM test in television can cost more than $50,000. Amounts like that can strain the budgets of many direct marketers, as well as tie up resources for an extended period of time.

Time spent testing in radio may increase the probability of success in the long run in other media. And if the test in radio proves successful, you not only will generate enough revenue to cover the cost of your test, but you may also decide to roll out your promotion in radio as well as your primary medium.

TESTING IN RADIO

When you test a promotion in radio, make sure that you are very thorough in your approach. Radio provides you with the flexibility to test a variety of approaches relatively inexpensively. If you plan to do an extensive roll-out, it only makes sense to cover all your bases during the testing period. Try as many of your creative approaches and appeals as possible. Change your price or your terms, or offer a premium. Try different markets, and different stations or program formats within those markets. Understand that your responses can be influenced by external factors that may be beyond your control but that you can take into consideration if you are aware of them. For example, warm weather or a sporting event on another channel (such as the Super Bowl) may significantly alter the composition of your audience, and artificially reduce responses to a promotion to below an acceptable level.

By the time you are finished, you should have accumulated enough information to be able to project response levels, weekly response patterns, and an accurate cost per order or lead for your roll-out.

START WITH RADIO

If you have never attempted television or radio EDM, radio EDM is probably the better medium in which to get your feet wet. If you have a background in direct marketing in the print media, the transfer into the electronic media can be smoother in radio than television. More of the direct marketing principles that you applied in the print media hold true with radio. With radio you still are concerned basically with copy; only the announcer will be reading the copy your audience would normally read in direct mail. Principles of audience targeting are also not dissimilar from direct-mail or space advertising.

Your direct-marketing budget may preclude your attempting a television EDM promotion. Most of your resources may be dedicated to direct marketing in the print media, and a large shift of resources may unnecessarily draw funds away from a profitable area.

You may not need the wide coverage of television in your promotion, especially if you have a product or service that can only be provided in a limited area. Health clubs, for example, have found success in attracting members with a combination of radio and telephone EDM. In another example, a rug cleaning company used radio EDM to sell their at-home rug cleaning service. In both of these examples television EDM would have been too expensive because the businesses would have had to pay to reach an audience that extended well beyond their service areas. Radio ads on local stations targeted their markets within those areas.

PRODUCTS

Radio has its limitations, and you should keep them in mind when considering radio and when preparing your radio promotions. First of all, radio is audio. The products you are selling cannot be seen. If it is absolutely necessary that your product be seen to be sold, radio is of course an inappropriate medium. For example, it would be difficult to sell a shirt or a pair of shoes using radio EDM. If your product requires visual demonstration to sell, it is probably inappropriate for radio EDM. It would be difficult, for example, to use the radio to demonstrate the dozens of wonderful things a blender can do.

Products that can take advantage of the audio dimension do quite well on radio. Records albums, for example, can be demonstrated by playing parts of various songs from the albums.

Just as in television EDM, your product cannot be too complex. Products or services that require a lengthy explanation will not do well on radio, especially if you attempt to use a one-step process. For example, insurance offers or services requiring a signature need to be promoted in a two-step process. You may be able to take a product that is selling well in the print media and convert it to radio or television EDM by simplifying it. For example, a book club that normally offers a wide selection of books to first-time buyers in print promotions offers a preselected library in its radio and television promotions.

Products that do well on radio take advantage of station formats. For example, news magazines, stock market services, and general merchandise do well on all-news stations. Retirement offers, insurance offers, albums, news magazines, general magazines, and general merchandise offers do well on classical music stations.

Your product may have a chance on radio no matter how unusual it might be. The disc jockey Wolfman Jack likes to recount stories of the various products he sold over the air when he worked early in his career at a radio station just south of the Texas border in Mexico. The station's broadcast coverage was well over the legal limit and reached into several Southwestern states. This coverage and Wolfman Jack's unique selling skills contributed to the success of many direct-marketing promotions. One of the most unusual and successful products Wolfman ever offered by direct response was live baby chicks. He sold thousands of them.

So don't be afraid to test your product on radio, and don't let others influence your decision to try radio if you feel there may be a market for it. The most reliable indicator of an EDM promotion's success or failure is through testing.

BUYING TIME

Buying time on radio is similar to buying time on television. Both radio and television are influenced by supply and demand and audience penetration levels. The highest rates are charged for programs or blocks of time with the largest audiences. With radio, most stations charge their highest rates during "drive time" periods in the morning and afternoon when consumers are commuting between work and home.

Most direct marketers find that EDM spots that are broadcast during these drive time periods do not generate enough response to make them worthwhile. The spots are expensive because they are highly rated, but response to EDM during drive time is either less than response to spots during other time periods, or cost per order is much higher. Part of the reason why there is low response during drive time is that consumers are either in their cars or not near a phone. They may not have access to a pencil and paper to write down the phone number or address from the offer. Even if they do manage to get the number or address down on paper, by the time they're near a phone, the impulse to respond to the offer is over, or they may have forgotten about the offer altogether.

Run of Station: Unless you are aiming for an audience within a particular program, you will want to purchase 60- to-120-second run-of-station (ROS) spots, a station's lowest published rates. The spots are scheduled by the station and immediately preemptible by advertisers paying full rates. Also, the more spots you purchase from a station, the lower the cost per spot is likely to be.

As in television, to gain the benefit of a full schedule, especially if it is a busy season, you may need to purchase as much as 150 percent more time than is really needed to compensate for preempted spots.

It is best to negotiate directly with stations for time purchases. You will more than likely be able to purchase time at less than station rates and you may also get an under the table agreement from the station to air your spot in day parts or adjacent to product-related programming.

If your credit rating is low or if you are a fledgling direct marketer and your credit rating is nonexistent, you may be required to pay cash up front for your spots. Some stations are cash poor; you may be able to use this problem to your advantage, however, by offering to pay cash up front as a condition for lower rates. Some marketers, even though they have good credit ratings, will do this to get better rates.

Per Inquiry: Per Inquiry (PI), where the station gets paid a predetermined rate for each order or lead instead of a fixed rate for time used, is much more prevalent in radio than in television. Before most stations will give you a PI deal, however, they will need to be convinced that your product will generate more revenue for them than other products or other promotions. You must first establish a track record, and to establish a record, you will need to initially purchase ROS or full-rate time spots. With those results in hand you will be better able to convince a station to use your promotion on a PI basis.

It is not advisable to use PI when you are testing. With PI it is difficult to keep track of where and how many times your spots were run. As a result, your target market and cost per order are difficult to determine.

Remember that if you have a promotion that really takes off, PI may end up costing you a lot more money than if you had purchased ROS or similar time spots; the more you sell, the more you pay the station. With set rates and a successful promotion, the money you pay to the station will not increase. PI is a safe way to go but increases your cost per order in successful promotions.

Some marketers have found that their best results from PIs are on clear channel stations—those that broadcast over wide areas of the country at night without interference from other stations.

Barter: It is sometimes possible to trade or barter a part of your inventory in exchange for air time. Barter is particularly useful if you have excess inventory or are low on cash. You can deal directly with the station or use bartering organizations to help to handle these transactions. The organization will place a value on your product and allow the station a certain amount of credit that it can use to obtain products (not necessarily your products) from the bartering organization.

R. David Thomas, the founder of Wendy's Hamburgers restaurant chain and the developer of the concept of Kentucky Fried Chicken restaurants, claims that he got the idea for Kentucky Fried Chicken restaurants as a result of a barter for radio time. At one time Thomas was strapped for cash and burdened with a failing restaurant. He exchanged some of the Colonel's chicken, which made up part of his restaurant's extensive menu, for some radio spots on a local station. Realizing that the chicken was the most popular item on the menu, he decided to specialize in just chicken, pared his menu to the "bone," and renamed his restaurant Colonel Sander's Kentucky Fried Chicken Take Home.

If you are considering barter, keep in mind that spots negotiated through bartering are usually preemptible. You may also find that the straight purchase of time from the same station would have given you more for your money, especially if the value placed on the goods you have bartered is questionable.

As in television EDM, you must test to find out if ROS, PI, barter, or other types of spots are best for your promotion. You may find that response to your promotion is highest and cost per order lowest from ads placed in highly rated programs or even during "drive time."

Radio Support: Radio is popular as support for direct marketing promotions in other media. A typical radio support spot is thirty seconds, much shorter than traditional 60- to 120-second direct-lead or direct-sale radio spots. Support ads will more than likely not contain a telephone number or address for response.

The emphasis on radio support is to ensure that the audience receiving your print media offer will also be reached with your radio ads. Because you will not be able to directly measure response from the spots, your primary concern in buying time will be the reach (R) and frequency (F) of your spots to ensure coverage. Coverage is determined by $R \times F = GRP$ or gross ratings points. Your time buys are usually made through station representatives rather than by dealing directly with the stations.

Make sure that the agency you choose for your campaign has experience in support EDM. Time buys for support promotions require an extensive knowledge of ratings systems as well as experience in measuring the impacts of support in the primary media.

Stations: Standard Rates and Data provides descriptive data for all stations in the United States. These data include information on program formats, areas of coverage, and rates.

CREATING THE SPOT

To sell on radio you must be able to convince the consumer to buy a product or service that he or she cannot see. But just because radio lacks the visual dimension does not mean that radio is limited in its ability to convey a message to the consumer or to get that consumer to respond. Radio capitalizes on the imagination. The "picture" of the product is created in the consumer's mind rather than on the television screen. Creative copy, background music, sound effects, and the announcer's delivery all can contribute to stimulating the imagination and persuading the consumer to respond.

Radio lets you be as creative as you want to be. Sound effects or background music, for example, can create the environment or setting, and put the consumer in the proper mood or frame of mind for your message. An ad for an investment magazine might use the background noise of a tickertape, an insurance offer may include the sound of children (dependents) playing, or Hawaiian music might accompany an EDM ad for trips to Hawaii.

Radio lets you demonstrate or describe your product. The best example is the playing of parts of several songs from a record offer.

Most of the time your copy and your announcer can do the describing. The consumer's imagination will do the rest.

The direct-marketing principles used for creating a radio EDM ad are basically the same as those in the print media and television EDM. First of all you must gain the attention of your target audience immediately. Music, sound effects, or a strong headline statement can be used to qualify the audience and grab its attention.

The headline should tell the audience why they should be listening to the ad. Make sure the headline is keyed toward those who can use your product or service. For example, with an insurance offer, the grabber might be: "If you were to die tomorrow, how would your family make ends meet?"

Within the body of the ad, interest can be developed by describing any benefits that the product or service will provide—security for the family, peace of mind, and so on. Any important features should also be mentioned—$250,000 coverage, that the policy can never be canceled, and so on. The end of your copy should have an action statement, a reason why the consumer should purchase or respond now and not wait—a limited offer, future price increases, a free gift, and so on. The end of your copy should contain all the details needed to purchase or respond—the telephone number, address, or other pertinent information. Be sure to include enough time for the announcer to clearly state and *restate* the ordering instructions. Your listeners do not have the benefit of seeing the number on the screen, or having both the address and telephone number displayed silently while the announcer is talking about something else. Many radio EDM ads begin with a statement such as the following; "Please have a pencil and paper ready for an important offer from XYZ Corporation."

Before airing the ad, have someone who has never heard your ad try to complete the ordering information.

PRODUCING THE SPOT

There are three basic ways a spot can be produced and aired: (1) The announcer can read live from a prepared script, (2) the announcer can ad-lib the spot, and (3) the spot can be produced in a studio to be aired later.

Live Script: The script read by the announcer can be very effective in generating responses. When the script is read live, the flow from regular programming into the ad is smooth. The announcer may be a sentence or two into the ad before the audience realizes that they are listening to an advertisement. By that time, however, their attention has been gained. A live ad may also sound like a personal endorsement of the product by the announcer. Many announcers develop large and loyal audiences that can be quite responsive to ads that the announcer reads, more so than a studio-produced tape with an unfamiliar voice.

An advantage of the live ad over a studio-produced tape is the speed with which changes can be made. The script can be rewritten quickly or changes can even be phoned in to the station, while changes to a studio-produced tape may take longer and be more expensive.

The marketer does not have as much control over the live ad as over a studio-produced tape. Each reading may be different from another; the announcer may sound as if he or she is reading the script, or may not be very enthusiastic, or the ordering information may be unclear.

Ad-lib: You may find that the ad-lib approach is best for your promotion. Instead of providing a structured script for the announcer to read, the announcer is just given basic information—a sample of the product, ordering information, or background information. The announcer creates the ad from there. The ad-lib can be quite effective, because the ad can sound spontaneous, natural, and most important, believable.

To ensure the effectiveness of the ad-lib or the live script spot, you may want to talk with the announcer personally about your product before he or she delivers the spots. Perhaps take the announcer to your place of business to show him or her how your business is run.

If the announcer really likes your product, he or she may become so enthusiastic about it that the planned one-minute spot turns into a two-minute spot, giving you an extra sixty seconds of free air time.

The ad-lib must be closely monitored. Since there is no script, you will have little control over the ad's structure. Make sure that the announcer understands the message that you want delivered to your audience, and that he or she spends enough time giving the details about how to order.

Studio-Produced Tape: The studio-produced tape gives you maximum control. You can be assured that your ad will be delivered the same way every time it is aired.

The studio tape frequently sounds more like an ad than the live script. The break between regular programming and the ad is more clearly defined, because the announcer for the regular programming and the announcer for the ad are usually different.

Response may be affected by the unfamiliarity of the voice touting the product. If at all possible, try to get an announcer from the same station where you will be airing the ad to record your spot. If you will be on several stations, a personality with a familiar or unique voice should be found to read the script. The cost for the personality's voice may be expensive, but possibly profitable for you in the long run.

Studio-produced tapes allow you to be the most creative. Special effects, music, and so on are easier to incorporate into the ad. You can rehearse the script and retape the spot several times until you are satisfied with it.

It is not difficult to find a studio to record your ad. Most radio stations are well equipped for commercial production and for a nominal fee can help you to record your ad. The studio-produced ad is more expensive than the live script: however, the cost is not prohibitive and is usually less than $500, including any creative assistance or consulting that may be needed.

Again, testing will indicate whether live script, ad-lib, or studio-produced tape is best for your promotion.

Summary of Important Points

Start with radio. Use it as your primary medium or to test promotions that will be used in other media.

Radio is inexpensive, flexible, personal, selective, and segmentable.

Most products can be sold with radio EDM as long as you recognize and compensate for radio's limitations. Capitalize on the imagination of the customer.

The negotiation and purchase of time is more flexible, and lead times are much shorter in radio than in other media.

The low cost of commercial production gives you an opportunity to test live script, ad-lib, or studio-produced formats, as well as various appeals.

6

THE TELEPHONE
AS AN INWARD
RESPONSE TOOL

Whether in combination with direct mail, catalogs, space ads, television, radio, or used by itself as a selling tool, the telephone plays a major role in the direct marketing process and is a driving force behind the explosive growth of the direct marketing industry.

Telephone marketing (telemarketing) is a technique that has come of age. Telemarketing is the use of the telephone to broaden or integrate sales or service functions. It is a system of placing or receiving telephone calls to capture orders, generate leads, and service existing customers, with the primary goal of making or increasing sales in a measurable and cost-effective manner.

The telephone has been used as a sales tool since its invention, but telephone marketing did not become a real factor as a multifaceted direct marketing tool until 1968 with the introduction of inward and outward Wide Area Telephone Service (WATS). Since then telemarketing has evolved into a multibillion-dollar industry. In 1983, industry experts estimate that more than $13 billion will be spent on the cost of telephone calls used in direct marketing promotions, up 15 percent from 1982.

IN WATS, which uses the toll-free "800" number, is used extensively for receiving orders from direct mail, catalogs, space ads, and television and radio EDM promotions. Non–direct marketing uses include dealer locator programs, which guide customers to nearest retail outlets; product information services; credit card authorization services; hotline input to nonprofit counseling and other organizations; and customer service assistance programs. OUT WATS uses include sales and research calls to consumers and businesses to sell products, develop leads, and service accounts.

The volume of toll-free calls placed in a year is staggering. AT&T estimates that in 1981, 1.6 billion toll-free calls were made, a 22 percent increase over 1980. A significant portion of these calls were either sales calls or calls where consumers placed an order. It has been estimated that the average household receives nineteen sales calls and makes sixteen calls to place an order per year. Business-to-business calls are estimated to be much greater.

There are several reasons why the telephone has become an important part of the direct marketing process.

The Telephone Is a Personal Medium. The telephone personalizes the direct-marketing process. With the telephone a two-way dialogue is created. Rather than dealing with an order form, most customers appreciate talking with a representative of your organization. Questions can be answered, problems resolved, and a generally more positive customer attitude about your company is created.

The Telephone Is Immediate and Convenient. Most direct-marketing promotions, and especially EDM promotions, rely upon an immediate consumer response. The longer a consumer waits after seeing a direct-response ad, the less likely that customer will be to respond. The effort of finding a pencil and paper, filling out an order form, addressing an envelope, and finding a stamp is an irritating procedure that can overcome the momentum created by all but the most compelling ads. The telephone is immediate. The consumer doesn't have to write anything down; he or she can pick up the phone and dial as the number is being flashed on the television screen. In a direct-mail campaign the number is printed for consumers. All that's needed is to pick up the phone and dial. The telephone makes ordering (responding) an effortless, painless, simple process.

On the other side of the coin, advertisers have been under increasing pressure to make their ads more results-oriented. A dollar spent on advertising should show an immediate, measurable return to justify its continuance. The telephone lets advertisers see at the end of each day the number of orders taken, the cost per order, the stations where the ad pulled best, and other pertinent information.

The Telephone Can Target Your Prospects. When used as an OUT WATS tool, the telephone can be as accurate as direct mail in pinpointing prospective customers. But the telephone can be more effective than direct mail in its ability to qualify prospects, generate leads, and close sales. When used as support to direct mail, the telephone can increase returns up to seven times that of direct mail alone.

The Telephone Can Save You Money. OUT WATS and IN WATS can be money savers. In a business-to-business environment, for example, OUT WATS used for prospect qualification, lead generation, and sales completions can considerably reduce the nearly $200 cost of the average industrial sales visit.

IN WATS can help advertisers make more efficient use of their money by pinpointing where ads are generating higher volumes and lower cost per order.

The Telephone Can Dramatically Increase Response. The telephone is more powerful than mail in average number of sales closed or leads generated per thousand attempts. For example, John Wyman, a marketing vice-president at AT&T reports (Sawyer, 1982) that of all responses to direct marketing promotions at AT&T, 58 percent are by mail and 42 percent by phone. However, *four times* as many sales are generated from customers who call.

IN WATS

Joseph Sugarman, author of the book *Success Forces* and president and founder of a very successful direct-marketing firm, claims to have been the first direct marketer to extensively use the "800" number as a response tool in direct marketing promotions. In the early 1970s, Sugarman found that the combination of the "800" number with space ads in the *Wall Street Journal* and other print media generated a response far above that previously achieved with address-only advertising.

Today the use of IN WATS has become popular as a tool used in combination with all forms of direct response media; it is now accepted as a response mechanism by the public and business community.

Increased public awareness of the toll-free "800" number is making it easier to get the public to respond by phone. An interesting example of toll-free response concerns viewers' reaction to an appeal to call a nonworking toll-free number. In the recent ABC movie *Pray TV* actor Ned Beatty played the part of a fictional preacher, Reverend Freddy Stone. At one point in the movie Beatty suggested that viewers call a toll-free number, 800-555-6864. The number was a nonworking number maintained by the telephone company and used in cases where a nonworking number is required. More than a few listeners responded to Beatty's request. The telephone company reported that Beatty's appeal generated more than 15,000 calls!

IN WATS AND THE PRINT MEDIA

Almost every catalog, direct-mail promotion, and space ad now includes a telephone number for response. Sears, for example, depends heavily on the use of the telephone for capturing orders. They report that 87 percent of their orders are by phone. Montgomery Ward reports a similar significant percentage (Simon, 1976).

Catalog houses report an overall greater level of response and a higher average order when the "800" number is included for response. Studies have shown that including the "800" number for response in the print media will increase response by 20 to 25 percent. Higher average orders are achieved in part because the telephone provides the opportunity to up-sell (persuade a consumer to purchase a more expensive item than the one originally ordered) or cross-sell (persuade a consumer to purchase products or services in addition to the item originally ordered).

Ways to Increase "800" Response

There are several things that you can do to encourage your customers' use of the "800" number. First, try to display the number as prominently and as frequently as possible in the ad. A space ad, for example, should have the "800" number displayed in the body of the ad and also within the coupon. If the coupon is clipped and another person sees the ad and wants to order the product, the number will still be there for response.

Many catalogs display an "800" number every few pages and combine it with a reminder to "call now."

It doesn't hurt to remind your customers that the call is free. Even though the majority of the population understand how the "800" number works, they may subconsciously regard the "800" number as a toll call. Besides, the word "free" is an excellent attention-getting device.

You should emphasize the days and hours that your number is available. If it is twenty-four hours, seven days a week, state that fact next to your number. You'd be surprised at the number of customers who call in their order outside of normal working hours. According to one expert, nearly 50 percent of all toll-free catalog orders come in after 5 P.M.

In-State Differences

Callers in the state where the "800" number service is based will not be able to call your interstate "800" number. Depending on the size of the population base within that state, you may elect to provide an intrastate number, a local number, or accept collect calls from your in-state customers. Either way, you will need to emphasize the in-state differences. But because the customer base for in-state response is usually smaller, you should not print the in-state number as large as your interstate number, and state the difference next to the number (for example, "if you live in Nebraska, call 800-xxx-xxxx"). You want to keep the size of the in-state number smaller than your interstate number to reduce confusion caused by interstate customers accidentally dialing the in-state number.

Another way to encourage telephone orders is to offer a premium, a gift, or discounts for telephone orders. Hall's Catalogs (Galginaitis, 1982), a catalog company owned by Hallmark Cards, encourages phone orders by advertising a catalog "special of the week" to customers who phone in their orders. The special not only encourages phone response, it also increases the average order per customer.

Television and Radio IN WATS

Less than a decade ago the primary response mechanism in the television and radio EDM ad was the address. Today the tables are reversed. The telephone number is found in nearly every EDM ad and is a major factor in the rapid growth of EDM. According to *Advertising Age* (1/18/82), during the peak month of January, more than 700 people dial an "800" number *every minute* in response to a television EDM commercial.

The telephone is a perfect companion to the EDM ad. The EDM ad is designed to motivate the consumer to "respond now"; the telephone allows that immediate response before the urge to order is diminished.

Should you use a telephone number, an address, or both in your television or radio ad? It is rare today for a television or radio EDM commercial to have only an address for response, but there are situations where an address only may pull better than telephone, or than telephone plus address. If your target audience is older, retirement age for example, response will generally be better with the address. The older generation apparently feels more comfortable responding by mail than by phone. This phenomenon may change as the current generation of middle-aged and younger people, more accustomed to responding by telephone, moves into the older-age categories.

Mail as response is good if you are trying to screen out unqualified responses. A request for payment, for example, increases the quality of your response even if quantity is less.

If you are advertising on radio, it is usually most effective to use either address or telephone, but not both. It is best to concentrate the seconds allocated to information about ordering on just one response vehicle to ensure that the consumer obtains that information. Without the aid of visual information it is more difficult for your audience to retain ordering information. Since the "800" number is usually simpler to remember and an easier means of response, more marketers are choosing its use.

The Address

An address may be appropriate if you do not have the facilities or the people for handling telephone response. If your budget is small, the cost of obtaining IN WATS lines or hiring a response-handling service may be too expensive for you.

You must remember that with the address, returns are much slower than telephone response. Your ability to assess the pull of your ads is made more difficult by this time lag. Time of day and response per spot information will be difficult to monitor. As a result, you will be limited in determining which spots are your most productive and which are your least productive. Your flexibility in making adjustments to take advantage of successful spots or eliminating poor spots is hindered.

If you decide to use an address, there are a few important details you will need to keep in mind. First of all, try to keep the address as uncomplicated as possible. Reduce the number of words that must be written or memorized. A shorter, simpler address not only makes it that much easier to remember, but it takes less time to say in your ad. You may be able to repeat the address three times in the same time it takes to repeat a longer, more complicated address once.

If your company is not well known, you should try to avoid the use of box numbers in your address. Box numbers give consumers the impression that your company is a fly-by-night operation. The consumer will be more reluctant to send his or her money to a box number. A full address gives customers a greater sense of permanence and helps them feel that they are mailing their money to a solid company.

Some radio and TV stations require that you use the station address for response. This is especially true in a per inquiry situation, so the station can keep track of the responses from your ads before forwarding them to you.

KEYING THE AD

You should key each of your ads so that you can keep track of where your mail is coming from. To key a telephone number, try varying it for each station. Otherwise you will need to instruct your order takers to request station information from your customers when they call.

For television, you'll need to provide a slide for each station. The slide should contain the address, price, guarantee, and any other necessary ordering information. At the bottom of the slide you will need to name the company sponsoring the promotion.

AD LENGTH

The length of your ad will influence the use of the address and telephone number in the ad. Generally, in a two-minute EDM ad, up to thirty seconds is allotted for ordering instructions. Thirty seconds is usually enough time to display and repeat both the telephone number and address in a television ad but may not be sufficient for a radio EDM ad, especially if the address and number are complicated. Even with a shorter commercial you should not skimp on the amount of time allotted to ordering instructions. A sixty-second commercial, for example, will probably require twenty seconds. An "800" number–only may be your best bet for the shorter EDM ad.

ORDERING INSTRUCTION VARIATIONS

There are several variations used for the presentation of the telephone number and address. Most ads reserve the final seconds for ordering instructions. Some ads will announce ordering instructions at the beginning and end of the ad. For example, an "800" number may be displayed on the screen and the announcer may say, "Please remember this number, 800-xxx-xxxx." Some television EDM ads for *Time* magazine mention the ordering instructions midway through the ad, continue with some more promotional information about the magazine, and then repeat the number in the final seconds.

Another effective way to get the customer to pick up the phone and dial is to actually show the announcer picking up the phone and dialing as he or she is saying the number.

No matter whether you use an address, telephone number, or both, you *must* ensure that your audience is given adequate opportunity to obtain the ordering information. Accurate transmittal of response instructions is crucial to the success of the EDM ad.

SETTING UP AN IN-HOUSE RESPONSE CENTER

You may be considering handling phone response in-house, but in most cases you will need to obtain the services of an outside response-handling agency. Most direct marketers lack the facilities for handling telephone response, especially phone response from television or radio EDM commercials. Response from television or radio EDM commercials can be erratic. For example, up to two thirds of the response from an EDM commercial comes within minutes of when the commercial is broadcast. This could be hundreds of calls in a very few minutes. If the phone lines are jammed, you've just lost a lot of business. The average customer will try the number once, and if it's busy, he or she will not try again.

On most roll-outs you can never be sure of the times when your commercial will air. Since most of your ads will probably be run-of-station, they could air any time in a twenty-four-hour period. If you aren't prepared for a twenty-four-hour operation, you should think about using a service.

If you have a catalog, space ad, or direct-mail operation, you might consider handling telephone orders in-house. Orders generally don't arrive in huge bursts as in an EDM promotion, so your operation will require fewer people in a less hectic environment. Most of your orders should be captured with less of a probability of jammed lines; however, you should still be prepared to attend to the phones outside of normal business hours.

If you decide to set up your own response center, you will need to contact your local telephone company. They can help you install their "800" number service. The number of lines and the level of "800" number service coverage depend upon the extent of your direct marketing operation.

How the "800" Number Service Works

The "800" number service works in the following way: With your state as the center, the country is broken into service areas, starting with the group of states surrounding your state. Depending on where you wish to do business, additional service areas (groups of states) can be added cumulatively until service includes all of the contiguous United States, Alaska, Hawaii, Puerto Rico, and the U.S. Virgin Islands. Rates for the service are based on hourly usage. The more hours the service is used, the lower the hourly rate. One-time-only charges are assessed for installation, and there is a monthly charge for each access line.

Toll-free interstate service does not include service within your own state. To receive intrastate toll-free, you will need to set up an additional line with a different toll-free number. Instead of setting up intrastate service, you might find it more advantageous to have your in-state customers call you collect. Or, if most of your customers within the state are within a local phone call area, you may just want to instruct those customers to dial your local number directly.

Order-Taking Procedures

Since you are paying rates based on usage, your order takers should work as quickly as possible. It is important, however, that courtesy and accurate order taking not be sacrificed for speed. Ordering information should include the following: (1) Where the advertisement was seen, including any keying information used in print ads, or the name of the broadcast station or telephone number used in the case of an EDM ad; (2) credit card information; (3) customer name, address (and delivery address if different), and phone number.

The amount of time spent on each order depends upon whether COD or credit is used, whether the caller has questions, or whether any cross-selling or up-selling will be used. Normally, to complete an order with a simple up-sell should take no longer than sixty to seventy-five seconds.

Up-Selling and Cross-Selling

The ability to up-sell or cross-sell is one of the advantages of an IN WATS operation. Studies have shown that these sales techniques can increase the average order by up to 40 percent.

An in-house staff is usually better qualified to up-sell or cross-sell because an in-house staff deals only with your company's product and is therefore in a much better position to handle questions, especially if the product or service is technical or complex. If the up-sell or cross-sell is not too complex, this can probably be handled by a national service.

Magazine publishers have for years increased the average length of their subscriptions by offering special rates to callers if they opt for a longer subscription than was advertised in the direct marketing promotion. Other up-sell techniques include offering discounts for volume purchases, specials of the week for telephone callers, or the deluxe model of the product. Cross-selling techniques include offering accessories to a product, or offering additional services if a customer calls on another matter. For example, when a customer calls in an order to a Sears store, the order taker will ask if the customer would like to open a Sears charge account. Or, if a customer calls an insurance company about a life insurance policy, the salesperson may ask if the customer would like to add auto insurance to his or her coverage.

THE OUTSIDE "800" NUMBER RESPONSE AGENCY

Most direct marketers involved in television and radio promotion and many direct marketers using the print media enlist the services of outside agencies to handle their telephone response.

There are many advantages to enlisting the services of an outside service agency. These agencies can save the time, trouble, and start-up cost associated with handling the response in-house, and they have the capability to handle the sporadic bursts of order activity generated by EDM commercials. As long as your product or service is not too technical and ordering is fairly straightforward and repetitive, a service agency can be a tremendous help to your operation. Most of these agencies are staffed around the clock with trained personnel capable of handling all types of response activity. These activities include handling direct purchases either by credit card or COD; requests for catalogs, literature, or samples; requests for a sales representative to return a call (lead capture); requests to register for meetings, seminars, and conventions; requests for the name of the nearest dealer/sales outlet; requests to enter contests or sweepstakes; any other response activity that might be generated from a toll-free promotion.

These agencies will also answer in the client's name; the consumer is not aware that a telephone response service is handling the order.

There are currently about twenty-five national agencies that handle direct marketing promotions. These agencies vary in size, and some specialize in one particular area of direct marketing. For example, not all agencies are experienced in handling EDM promotions.

Since intrastate "800" service is not used extensively, most agencies are located in states with low population centers (Nebraska, Missouri, Nevada). If intrastate service is not used, the potential loss of a market is relatively small. If it is used, fewer customers will need to note the different number.

Choosing the Response Agency

The choice of a response agency is important. There are several factors you should consider and questions that should be asked: How many telephones are available for response? How many of those phones are staffed? How much of a load is there on each staffed phone? How quickly can the service expand its phones or staff in the event of a successful roll-out?

Get a list of references and clients from the agency. Call some of the clients and ask about the service. Were they satisfied with the service? Call in an order to the agency from a client's current promotion. Was the order taker courteous and efficient? The quality of the staff should be consistent. There should be no exceptions. If you have a problem with an order taker, look elsewhere.

Does the agency have any experience in your media? Can they up-sell or cross-sell?

Finally, if at all possible, visit a center or two. Familiarize yourself with their operations. Are you compatible with their management and personnel?

Depending on the size and success of your promotion, you should consider either lining up a backup agency or using two agencies concurrently. There are two reasons for this. First, if your promotion is a success, a large roll-out may overload the lines of one agency. Using two agencies will help to reduce your busy signal ratio. Second, if you find in the middle of a promotion that the service you are receiving from an agency is poor, or if the agency goes out of business, you will still have a backup supplier. The IN WATS service agency field is extremely volatile. It is difficult for an agency to predict incoming call volumes and staffing requirements, and competition for direct marketers' business is intense. One expert in the telephone response field predicts that in the next several years the current number of national service agencies will be reduced from twenty five to ten. Be very careful and thorough when choosing an agency.

Order-Taking Innovations

Some agencies are better equipped to handle responses efficiently than others. For example, some agencies use the computer and cathode ray tube (CRT) to perform functions that include storing and retrieving product information, credit card verification, inventory control, and address verification.

With the use of computer software, order-taking speed can increase dramatically. Increased order speed can have a significant effect on cost savings. For example, a drop of four seconds on a one-minute order would result in a sales increase of almost 7 percent without increasing labor cost.

There are other order-taking innovations that should be available soon. WATS Marketing of America, for example, will soon be able to transfer funds from a customer's account instantly and directly into the advertiser's account.

Agency Rates

Most agencies structure their rates along similar lines. There is usually a one-time setup charge of from $200 to $500, depending on the media used, and an advance payment of several hundred dollars is usually required. Additional charges are levied on a per order basis, with discounts given as the number of orders increases. Per order charges range from less than $1 for high-volume orders to more than $2 for low-volume or more complex orders, such as credit card orders.

Locating an Agency

There are several sources that will provide addresses and phone numbers of the agencies. Your public library should have copies of *Advertising Age* or *Direct Marketing* magazine. The agencies usually advertise their services in these publications. If you are working with a direct response advertising agency, they may be able to recommend a suitable response-handling agency. The Direct Mail/Marketing Association can provide an up-to-date list of agencies. Their address is: DMMA, 6 East 43rd Street, New York, NY, 10017. The following list includes the names and addresses of a few of the larger agencies. It is also possible that another or a smaller service may be right for your promotion.

Team Telephone, 9222 Bedford Ave., Omaha, Nebraska, 68134. 800-228-2258

USA 800, 5521 Raytown Road, P.O. Box 16795, Kansas City, Missouri, 64133. 800-821-2280

WATS Marketing of America. 800-228-2228.

Using a Local Service

If you plan a direct-marketing promotion that will not extend beyond a local area or will remain within a state, you may want to consider utilizing the services of a local telephone answering service. Local answering services are not usually equipped to handle the same large volumes of response as a national service, but they can provide acceptable service if volumes are expected to come in somewhat uniformly. Usually, however, only the larger local answering services have had experience in handling responses from direct marketing promotions. Be sure to check them out thoroughly before using them. Don't be surprised if a local service claims they can handle your projected volume of orders. Many of these answering services are staffed with competent personnel who have had years of experience in handling local direct-marketing promotions and can rival the national agencies in the varieties of services they provide.

Summary of Important Points

The telephone has been the driving force behind the growth of EDM and other direct marketing methods.

The telephone is personal, immediate, convenient, and affordable. It can target your prospects. More important, it can dramatically increase response to your promotions.

Increased consumer awareness of the "800" number has contributed to the success of direct marketing promotions.

IN WATS is used in conjunction with the majority of direct marketing promotions in the print and electronic media.

Always give the customer adequate time to obtain ordering information.

An in-house order-taking facility is appropriate for mail-order or catalog operations.

Order taking should be done accurately and quickly. Reduction of order taking time is important in a high-volume promotion.

Cross-selling and up-selling can increase returns by as much as 40 percent.

Choose an outside agency carefully. Match their experience to your needs.

7

OUTWARD TELEPHONE MARKETING

The first large-scale telephone marketing campaign occurred in the 1960s. To stimulate slumping sales, Ford Motor Company launched a massive telephone campaign designed to generate leads for their salespeople. During the course of the campaign more than 20 million telephone calls were placed, and enough leads were obtained to give 34,000 salespeople two leads a day for thirty days. Sales increased and the slump was reversed.

Since the 1960s, use of the telephone as a sales tool has increased dramatically. More and more businesses are discovering that the telephone can be their most responsive and most cost-effective sales tool.

Three major factors have contributed to increased use of the telephone for marketing.

Attention: The telephone more than any other medium has the ability to capture and hold the attention of the listener. Most individuals feel obligated to answer the phone. They will interrupt a busy schedule to respond to a call. Once on the line, the opportunity for one-on-one selling exists; the sales message can be presented, and objections can be met and overcome.

Cost: In the first chapter we mentioned that sales visits can be extremely expensive, especially in an industrial sales environment where one visit can cost about $200, and where several visits are usually required to generate a sale. Telephone calls, in contrast, are less expensive and can sometimes be just as effective as a personal visit. Direct mail and other print media may be much less expensive than telephone per contact, but may be less effective than the telephone in their ability to generate response.

Productivity: Studies have shown that the average salesperson wastes up to 70 percent of a sales day in travel time and waiting in customers' offices. In the time it takes to visit five or six customers personally, the telephone salesperson can contact twenty-five or thirty. The sales-attempt–to–sales ratio may be higher with a personal sales visit, but usually the higher number of calls that can be made by telephone more than compensates for the lower ratio.

TELEPHONE SELLING TECHNIQUES

Even though telephone marketing is experiencing newfound popularity and rapid growth, the majority of businesses today still do not use the telephone as a selling tool, and the majority of those that do are not using the telephone as effectively as they could. There are a multitude of ways that the telephone can be used to increase sales, and one or more of them can probably be applied to your sales mix. Following are some examples.

Direct Sales: Make sales directly over the phone. This is easiest to do when you have an established customer base. Your customers have ordered from you before and will not be as apprehensive about ordering over the telephone. Don't be afraid to experiment with this. You'll be surprised how many of your customers will respond to a telephone call.

Another technique you might try is to schedule your sales visits to your customers further apart—once every six months, for example, instead of once every three months. On the third month contact your customers by phone. If your customers know you will be using the telephone, this can be an effective way to do business. You will not only be able to cover your territory or customer base in about 10 percent of the time it takes to travel to each one; the additional time you will have available will also allow you to prospect for and serve new customers.

Direct-Sell Any Product or Service. There probably has never been a product that has not been sold by telephone. One woman even successfully negotiated the sale of a jet airplane by telephone. Whether you are selling to businesses or to the general public, the telephone probably has application to your business as a primary or secondary sales tool.

Some companies rely almost totally on the telephone as their sales and order capture tool. Olin Mills Portrait Studios, for example, is one of the pioneers of telephone selling. They use the telephone almost exclusively to attract nearly 3.5 million customers a year to their photography studios for family and individual portraits.

Should You Use the Telephone? How heavily should you rely on the telephone? Burdened by high outside sales costs and a slow economy, many businesses report that they have converted their field sales forces to in-house telephone salespeople, and that the conversions usually resulted in an increase of accounts.

If you switch to a telephone sales operation, you may experience an initial loss of some of your older accounts, but the increased number of contacts that can be made and the new accounts that can be generated by telephone will more than make up for the loss.

The conversion to telephone can also be made much smoother by informing your customers of the impending change in selling operations. Most of your customers will appreciate the switch, especially if they understand that you will be saving money and time by going to a telephone operation, and that those savings can be passed along in price reductions or price freezes to them. You may also be pleasantly surprised to find that many of your customers will welcome the change. Many purchasing managers, for example, prefer purchasing products over the telephone.

Expand Your Market Base. Instead of opening a new retail or wholesale outlet to gain new customers, and allocating an excessive amount of capital and time to do so, many businesses are expanding their customer bases through the use of the telephone. One West Coast tire and tire accessory distributor, for example, was contemplating opening another outlet in the Midwest but found that the capital commitment was beyond his immediate means. So he instead hired two telephone salespeople to contact retail outlets in the Midwest. The telephone operation proved so successful that more salespeople were hired. The business now has accounts throughout the United States.

Lead Development: Develop leads for your salespeople with the telephone. Many businesses now have full-time telephone staffs assigned to generate leads for their field salespeople. The salespeople can devote 100 percent of their time to selling because each sales lead has been qualified by the telephone staffs before the sales appointment. Each sales call is therefore more productive.

One distributor of insulated windows, who had his telephone staff acquire and qualify leads for his salespeople, reported a sale–to–sales–call ratio of nearly 50 percent.

An American Telephone and Telegraph Corporation campaign that invited prospects to a new-product demonstration for NCR Corporation attracted 24 percent of the prospects called.

A telephone campaign for Bell and Howell's business equipment group made sales appointments with 35 percent of the persons on their prospect list ("Telephone Marketing Demanding Increased Attention," 1977).

Eliminate Cold Calls: Instead of knocking on doors and making cold calls, use the telephone. One expert calls this "ringing telephone bells instead of doorbells." When you use the telephone, you bypass the corporate structure that so often frustrates salespeople. Most businesses feel obligated to answer the phone and deal with your questions. The telephone not only lets you get your foot in the door, but also lets you avoid cooling your heels with other salespeople in an outer office; you have an established appointment with an individual who knows who you are and why you are there. The agony of the face-to-face cold call, dreaded by so many salespeople, can now be avoided.

Prospecting by telephone can save you lots of time. A West Coast telephone company marketing representative reported that one of her clients was flying regularly to Alaska to make cold calls (forgive the pun). After consultation it was found that the salesperson was able to eliminate a substantial amount of time and cost by using the telephone to sell to a majority of his potential customers.

Call Ahead: Reserve one day a week to make appointments for the rest of the week. You'll be more organized, save time, and be able to see more of your customers.

Business Contacts: Sales opportunities are lost when you communicate with your customers by letter. Rather than sending a letter to a customer, if at all possible make a telephone call instead. Not only will you save the time and cost of preparing a letter (McGraw-Hill estimates that it now costs, on the average, more than $7 to prepare and mail a letter), but a telephone call also gives you an opportunity to reestablish personal contact, to assess your customers' needs, and to capture additional orders.

Marginal Customers: Use the telephone to contact marginal customers that you otherwise could not afford to see. You may have small customers not far away from your larger accounts or customers who you are not sure will place an order if you do make a sales visit. Many salespeople are finding it profitable to visit their marginal accounts on a less-frequent basis than larger accounts and will call instead to take orders. A salesperson traveling through a large metropolitan area, for example, can visit larger accounts personally and call the marginal ones. Much time can be saved, and marginal accounts can be kept alive or even developed into profitable ones.

Open a New Territory. If you are opening a new sales territory or reopening a long ignored one, use the telephone to make your initial customer contacts. It will take you much less time to establish yourself and to make your territory self-sufficient. One office supply salesperson reported that with the help of two telephone salespeople, a new two-state territory was established in one third of the time used to reopen a similarly sized territory without telephone assistance.

Reestablish Old Accounts. Maintain contacts with customers who for one reason or another have stopped ordering from you: "Hello, Bob. Just wanted to say hello and let you know that whenever you need more of our product, we're here to help you. We believe that we can be as competitive on price as any of your other suppliers, and you know that we have the best service in the state. If you have any questions, please let me know. In the meantime, I'd like to check back periodically to see how you're doing."

Secure Reorders. Maintain a dated file of customer orders and inventory levels. Contact your customers at regular intervals when you know inventory levels will be depleted and new products will need to be ordered.

Conversions: Convert your trial customers to permanent customers. For example, you can leave your product with customers on a trial basis and, at a later date, call to close the sale by phone.

Up-Sell and Cross-Sell: Many businesses that receive orders for products will call their customers back and try to up-sell or cross-sell them. For example, a deluxe edition of the same product could be offered, a special price could be offered for volume purchases, or accessories to the product could be sold: "Thank you for your order, Mrs. Smith. I just called to tell you that we are now producing a deluxe version of our widget and we're having a special introductory price reduction that I was sure you would like to take advantage of."

88

An out-of-stock condition can be a sales opportunity for you. Perhaps you have another product that would do the job just as well. Instead of sending an out-of-stock notice, call the customer and offer the alternative product.

Telephone Support of Other Media: Use the telephone to back up direct-mail campaigns, ads in trade magazines, or personal sales visits. The combination of two or more media can be a powerful sales generator. Telephone support of direct mail, for example, can be an average of three to four times more effective than direct mail alone.

One telephone sales technique that generates good results is to mail a letter to a potential customer that describes the features and benefits of your company's product. The end of the letter includes a statement saying that you will call on a certain date and time to further explain the product.

Media Support of Your Telephone Promotion: You can also use other media to support your telephone efforts. Most good salespeople realize that many times sales are not made on the first customer contact. Additional calls or other forms of contact are sometimes needed to make a sale. One popular method used to increase sales is to follow up the telephone contact with a letter thanking the potential customer for his or her time, even if the initial phone call did not produce an order. Not only does the follow-up letter foster good will between the potential customer and the salesperson, but also the customer may be more inclined to order the next time a telephone contact is made.

Handle Response From Other Media: Leads produced from print or broadcast campaigns can be handled by telephone. A Texas-based company that sells motivational courses and franchises produces leads from space ads that offer a free motivational cassette tape. Salespeople later call these leads to assess the degree of interest in the product, and either close the sale over the phone or have the potential customers travel to the company's headquarters for the "close."

Service: An area of concern to customers is the level of service that can be provided by telephone. You must take steps to assure your customers that service will not suffer when dealing with them by telephone. With the telephone you can check on your customers more frequently to determine if service is acceptable, to solve service problems, or to answer service-related questions. The service call also provides an opportunity to assess current inventory levels and negotiate additional sales.

THE SCRIPT

In many selling situations it will be necessary for you to prepare a script for your salespeople to follow. Scripts are appropriate in those sales and lead-generation promotions where a structured or repetitive sales message is required.

The script has several advantages over the nonscripted sales message. Scripts provide consistency and control. They ensure that the same message is delivered every time. With a script, nothing is inadvertently forgotten; guarantees, special offers, ordering information, benefits, and so on are all presented exactly as you want them to be presented.

Scripts save time. Their structure ensures that your salespeople do not ramble or waste valuable telephone time.

Less training is usually required when you use a script. Labor costs are lower because less special selling skills are required of the salespeople. You also will have a much larger labor pool from which to draw.

Script Structure: Your script should be composed of five basic parts: introduction, qualification, sales message, close, and order, or lead, capture.

The introduction should include your company's name, your name, and a question asking for confirmation of the name of the customer.

The next part of your script should qualify the customer. Is he or she interested in your product or service?

Once the customer is qualified, the script should lead into the sales message. Benefits should be stressed. What can the product or service do for the customer?

The close may be as simple as asking the customer if he or she would like to purchase the product: "Would you like to try our product for a 30-day no obligation trial?" "When would be the best time for one of our salespeople to call, Mr. Jones?"

Once confirmation of an order or lead is received, it is important to take down the order accurately and completely. If a credit card is involved, for example, have the customer read back the number to you. Make sure the customer understands that he or she has just purchased a product or agreed to a sales appointment. Read back the information that was just taken down; this helps to reconfirm the agreement: "Mr. Jones, I'll arrange for a salesperson to call on you at your home at two hundred twenty-two Sharon Drive, five o'clock, June twenty-third. Thank you very much for your time, Mr. Jones."

Under almost no circumstances should your salespeople be allowed to improvise or deviate from the script. Well-written scripts anticipate all responses from the customer, including questions and objections, with a written response that the salesperson can read. In a way the script can be thought of as a tree with many branches. Customer questions or objections determine to which branches of the script the salesperson goes. Each response to a question or objection is designed to lead the customer back to the trunk or main part of the sales message and into the close. For example, if the customer says that the product is too expensive to pay for all at once, the telephone salesperson would move to the written response to that objection: "Yes, Mr. Jones, most of our customers are unable to pay for our product in one payment. That's why we have an installment plan available that lets you make monthly payments for up to two years. And you don't have to start paying any interest for six months. So if you pay for our product before the sixth month, it doesn't cost you anything extra! Now, would the afternoon or evening be a better time for one of our salespeople to call?"

Depending on the product or service, the potential list of questions and objections could be quite lengthy. The script, therefore, may be several pages long. The salesperson may only use a small part of the script during any one call. But the more potential questions and objections there may be, the more reason there is to have a script that anticipates them. Instead of being overwhelmed by too many variables, the salesperson simply turns to the response, reads it, and leads the customer back to the sales message.

The script should be written so that it can be read in a conversational tone. When read verbatim, the script should not sound contrived or stiff to the customer. The salesperson can help to affect this by reading the script in a natural, spontaneous manner. The customer should never be aware that the salesperson is reading from a script. (See 'Sample Script' at the end of this chapter.)

UNSCRIPTED SELLING

The prepared script is inappropriate in some telephone selling situations. Most business-to-business sales calls, for example, are made without the use of a script. Business-to-business calls are usually more personalized or individualized than calls to consumers. The salesperson and the customer may very likely do business on a regular basis; the scope of the conversation may include comments about family and friends as well as the state of the economy, and so on. A script trying to capture all the variables in a personalized selling environment would be hopelessly complex and unwieldy.

Other situations where a script may not be the best approach include the sale of complex, technical products or high-priced, low-volume items requiring a less repetitive, more personalized explanation or several telephone calls to close the sale. The woman who negotiated the sale of the jet airplane, for example, most certainly did not work from a script.

Prepare Thoroughly

Working without a script does not mean that the salesperson can just pick up the telephone and dial. Successful telephone selling requires a considerable amount of precall preparation. There are several things you or your salespeople can do to prepare for the sales call. To begin with, you must be aware of your customers' buying patterns. If you are calling a customer for a reorder, for example, you should have kept dated records indicating when stock should be replenished. If you call at the wrong point in the customer's buying cycle, you will have wasted a call and irritated the customer.

Even though you may not use a script, thorough preparation should result in a detailed outline that will guide your sales presentation. Your presentation should include the following: an opening statement introducing yourself and your company; qualification of the customer to determine whether he or she is the appropriate individual to hear about your product (in a business-to-business call you may need to go through several people before you reach the right one); presentation of the sales message (stress the benefits of your product or service and involve the customer in your message to monitor interest levels); closing of the sale and summary of the order, or arranging for a future sales call.

Practice your sales message several times alone or with a fellow salesperson before calling your first customer. Speak slowly, clearly, and confidently. Make your tone of voice bright and positive.

Message Length

Although it depends on the product, your sales message should not last longer than four to five minutes. Remember, you are cutting into your customers' day, possibly interrupting them from important meetings or projects. Lengthier messages will only irritate your customers or have to be cut short before you can close the sale.

Know Your Product Backward and Forward. What are its benefits? What can it do for the customer? What are the features that create those benefits? Anticipate questions. Make a list of potential questions your customer might ask, and write down or memorize the answers to all of the questions before you call. Keep handy all of your price lists, statistics, inventory information, and so on. Quick response to customer questions makes you appear confident and knowledgeable to the customer. When you can't answer a question, you not only put doubt in the customer's mind about your credibility and competence; you also put control of the conversation back into the hands of the customer.

Anticipate Objections. It is almost a given that in every one of your sales calls the customer will voice an objection to purchasing your product. Most objections fall into the following categories: The customer doesn't have the money or thinks the price is too high; doesn't like the product; doesn't need the product; would like to buy some other time but not now. Be ready with responses to those objections or any others that you think the customer might come up with. For example: "I can appreciate your wanting to wait until next quarter to buy, Mr. Smith. But we are offering a 'three for the price of two' special this month only, and I'd hate to see you pay full price for the same items next quarter. Don't you agree?"

Listen to What the Customer Has to Say. Telephone selling is two-way communication. You can learn to size up customer attitude by the tone of the voice. Is he or she responsive to your questions? Is he or she interested in what you have to say? Your customer's responses will have an effect on the direction of your conversation. For example, if you are a poor listener, you may miss verbal cues indicating that the customer is ready to buy, even though you are only part of the way through your presentation. If you ignore these cues, you may miss the opportunity to close the sale, an opportunity that may disappear by the end of your presentation because the customer may have lost interest or changed his or her mind.

PRERECORDED SALES MESSAGES

A telemarketing practice that is becoming increasingly popular is the use of prerecorded messages to obtain leads and to sell products or services. Prerecorded messages are delivered in two basic ways: with operator assistance, or with automatic dialing and recorded message players (ADRMPs).

With the operator-assisted recorded message, the salesperson dials a sales prospect and introduces himself or herself and the company he or she represents. The operator will then ask permission to play a recorded message about the product or service. The message may be delivered by the president of the company, a recognizable entertainment personality, or a respected authority on the product or service; it may include testimonials from satisfied customers. When the message is completed, the operator comes back on the line to ask for the order or to set up an appointment for a salesperson to meet with the customer.

ADRMPs, first introduced in 1977, do not require human intervention to operate. ADRMPs are set up to self-dial from eighty to 100 telephone numbers per hour in a sequential pattern within a prefix. When the customer answers, the machine, which can be voice activated, responds by announcing that the message the customer is about to hear is prerecorded, explains the purpose of the message, and asks for the customer to continue listening. At this point the customer has the option either to listen or to hang up the phone, thereby terminating the call. If the customer listens to the message and decides to respond, order capture can occur in two ways. If the system is fully automated, it may operate similar to an answering machine; that is, the customer leaves his or her name or telephone number for later follow-up. Or, the customer may be told that if he or she wants to order or respond to please stay on the line. The operator then comes on the line and captures the order or sets up an appointment.

Product and Service Application

The recorded message has potential application to hundreds of different business areas. Millions of calls are now placed each year by dozens of businesses. Real estate and insurance firms, financial institutions, and publishers like *Encyclopedia Britannica* are using recordings to develop leads for their salespeople. Others, like Standard and Poor's, *Reader's Digest*, Dreyfus Corporation, and *Women's Wear Daily* are using this method to capture orders directly.

Benefits

Recorded messages provide a uniformity and consistency that cannot be matched by a live scripted or unscripted sales message. Recordings are tireless. The tone and intent of the message never varies, regardless of the number of calls made.

The credibility of your sales message is enhanced and the customer more inclined to listen and order when your spokesperson is your company president or a satisfied customer with a testimonial.

Your training and labor costs should be less with a promotion that uses recordings. Since most of the sales message is usually delivered within the recorded part of the presentation, the operator need only be trained to introduce the tape, answer questions and objections, take down order information, or set up sales appointments.

Negative Consumer Reaction

Although promotions that use recordings are becoming increasingly popular, there has been some negative consumer reaction to the use of ADRMPs. When ADRMPs were introduced, a great deal of controversy arose about their potential for invasion of privacy. This controversy was heightened by the fact that the first ADRMPs had two technical features that caused a great deal of customer irritation.

First of all, ADRMPs are programmed to dial telephone numbers in a sequential pattern. This means that the systems do not discriminate between listed and unlisted telephone numbers. Many people with unlisted numbers did not appreciate being called with a sales message.

Second, some of the earlier ADRMPs, after seizing the line, did not disconnect until the entire sales message was completed, even if the customer hung up the telephone in the middle of the message. This was irritating to listeners who needed to make immediate outgoing telephone calls. The Direct Mail Marketing Association has recently established guidelines recommending that ADRMPs not be used unless the telephone immediately disconnects after the customer hangs up.

Most consumers prefer the messages that combine operator and tape over messages that use tape only. Tape-only promotions, without the personalized touch that the operator provides, can be irritating and annoying to consumers. For this reason, tape-only promotions have a more limited application than those that are operator assisted.

The use of recorded messages in telephone promotions will continue to be popular. However, promotions that use taped messages, and especially promotions that use tape without operator intervention should be developed with care and monitored closely to ensure that the consumer will not be offended.

TIMES TO CALL

Knowing the right day and time to call your customers will reduce the average number of call attempts per customer and result in a more effective use of telephone selling time.

The right time to call your customers is determined by common courtesy and a knowledge of your target audience. Certain times of the day and days of the week are better than others for calling customers, and there are certain times that should be avoided altogether. For example, you should never call too early in the morning or too late in the evening. A general rule of thumb is to call between 9 A.M. and 9 P.M. You may be able to contact more of your customers earlier or later than these times, but your customers will more than likely still be asleep or retiring for the evening. You should also be sensitive to religious customs. Seventh Day Adventists, for example, should not be called on a Saturday, and no telephone sales calls should be made on Sunday.

Business-to-business contacts should be made during business hours, of course. Sometimes response is best early in the morning or late in the afternoon when most executives are preparing for the day or returning to the office from meetings to receive messages. Expect that a large portion of business calls will require several attempts to get through to the decision maker.

The best times to call consumers will vary, depending upon the audience you are trying to reach. For example, one telephone marketer has a target audience of married housewives with children. The marketer found that the best times to reach this audience were between 9 A.M. and 1 P.M., and between 4 P.M. and 8 P.M. Calls between 1 P.M. and 4 P.M. were discovered to be unproductive because by 1 P.M. most of the customers were out of the house either shopping or on errands.

Weather is also a factor that can influence calling contacts. For example, if the weather is nice, mornings and evenings are more productive calling times, because most people will be out of their homes in the afternoons.

A minimum of four callbacks should be made to reach nonanswers. It may be that the customer is never home during certain parts of the day. You should vary the time of your callbacks to increase the probability of reaching these customers. If you do reach a member of a household and have determined that the person you are trying to reach is not available, simply ask the person to whom you are speaking for an appropriate callback time.

HIRING AND TRAINING

It is not necessarily true that an individual who is successful at face-to-face selling will be a successful telephone salesperson. This is because a large part of face-to-face selling is nonverbal. In fact, some experts estimate that up to 70 percent of communication is nonverbal. The wink of an eye, a firm handshake, facial expressions, body posture, and so on, can all play a role in transmitting the face-to-face sales message and influencing customer response. The telephone salesperson, on the other hand, must rely almost completely upon verbal communication. The customer's impression of you and your company is based on a disembodied voice at the other end of a telephone line. In the space of only a few minutes the telephone marketer must gain the trust of the customer and convince that customer to buy a product or service from a complete stranger.

Selecting Your Salespeople

Proper selection and training of your salespeople is important. You should select your people for their ability to communicate verbally and not let yourself be influenced by nonverbal cues or physical appearance.

To best avoid nonverbal impressions, it is advisable to interview all of your potential salespeople by telephone. This way you will not be influenced by any nonverbal skills they may possess. Instead, you must base your impressions on their speaking ability. You will be surprised how well this interviewing technique works.

Have the applicant read something to you, such as an article in the newspaper. For consistency, have them all read your classified ad. Does the person speak clearly? Is he or she easy to understand? Is the voice pleasing, or is it monotone or irritating? Does he or she sound "friendly"? Would you consider buying a product or service from this person?

There are other personal attributes that contribute to successful telephone selling. For example, your salespeople must have the patience to handle a repetitive task, as well as the ability to continually bounce back from no-sale situations.

If you are considering your field salespeople for telephone marketing psoitions, you should put them through this same interviewing process. It will quickly become obvious if your field people have good telephone presence. If not, retraining will be necessary before you can expect them to be as successful on the phone as they are in the field.

Training Length

The extent of your training efforts will be dependent on several factors. Training will take longer if the product is complex or highly technical, if the offer is complicated, and especially if you are not using a script. Other factors influencing training include relative past sales and telephone sales experience and the complexity of the telephone equipment. For example, you may be using computers and CRTs, which may take some time to master.

Selling Style

Hard-sell high-pressure sales techniques do not work with the telephone and are not recommended. A more subtle sales approach produces better results. Training should emphasize a natural, spontaneous conversational style delivered with a pleasant-sounding speaking voice. Some experts suggest that you tell your salespeople to smile while talking. Smiling can make the tone of the voice more pleasing and positive sounding.

OUTSIDE TELEPHONE MARKETING SERVICES

You may decide to hire an outside firm to perform telephone marketing functions for you. But before you do, you should carefully consider the positives and negatives of hiring an outside firm over performing the function in-house.

In-House Advantages

An in-house telephone marketing operation has its advantages. In the first place you may already have a field sales force knowledgeable about your products or services. Depending on the complexities of the product, that knowledge may have taken many months to acquire. In addition, your field sales force may have already developed a strong list of customers from field sales activity. It may be a simple matter to train your salespeople to sell to those customers by telephone instead of face-to-face. Most important, maintaining an in-house operation gives you more control of the selling environment than with an outside agency.

Outside Service Advantages

There are many situations, however, when you will want to consider the outside firm. If you are planning to run a short-term product promotion with the telephone, you may not want to commit to the funding that a longer-term in-house telephone selling operation may require. If you want to get started on a project in a relatively short time, an outside firm can usually be on-line much faster.

The outside firm can perform a variety of outward-selling services, from the simplest repetitive tasks to complex selling situations. Outside firms are usually best at handling promotions requiring a high volume of repetitive calls or lead-generating tasks requiring moderate amounts of training of their sales staffs. These staffs usually work from prepared scripts or detailed outlines with little individual variation.

You might want to consider using an outside service, for example, to generate leads for your field sales force. Or you might want to use a service for a test promotion. Tightly controlled and precisely measured tests can be performed, with short start-up times and no long commitments from you.

Remember that once you have chosen the outside firm, you are relinquishing control of the sales or lead process to that firm, and it will represent itself as your company in its contacts. Make your choice with care.

Outside services will provide you with cost figures that cover all of their expenses, including overhead and an amount for their profit. In addition to start-up fees, charges are usually levied on a per call basis. You can compare these cost figures with estimates of what it would take to perform the same function in-house. Cost, however, should not be the only basis for comparison. The advantages of the short lead times of an outside service, for example, may outweigh a cost differential that favors an in-house operation.

Even if you decide to use in-house staff, the outside agency can be useful. Some agencies will provide consultation to assist with setting up an in-house telemarketing promotion or operation and will train your salespeople.

Another good source for assistance is your local telephone company. Most local companies provide Phone Power consultants to businesses who either intend to start an in-house operation or who want to increase the effectiveness of an already established telephone sales force. These consultants can help you in many ways. They can help estimate costs, advise you on the number of lines you might need, formulate the ideal size of your sales force, help you in hiring the right salespeople, develop compensation programs, and provide training classes. Best of all, this help is inexpensive—in many cases, free. Compensation to the telephone company is the increased use of your telephone.

TIME-LIFE LIBRARIES, INC.

(Information on the Time-Life Libraries, Inc., telephone marketing operation was graciously provided by Robert B. Doell, branch manager for Time-Life Libraries, Inc.)

A good example of a well-run telephone marketing operation is Time-Life Libraries, Inc., the telephone marketing arm of Time-Life Books, Inc. Time-Life Libraries operates in four regional offices strategically located across the United States. Three offices concentrate on new sales, and the fourth, the national sales office, concentrates on renewals from current customers.

Each office covers a several-state area of the United States and Canada, using WATS, local, foreign exchange, and independent interconnect telephone services. Customer names come from several different sources, including lists of *Time, Life, Sports Illustrated*, and *People* subscribers and from telephone books, and are screened by zip code and by income bracket to ensure quality. Lists of subscribers are used sparingly. That is, an interval of time up to a year will pass before more than one telephone contact is made, partly out of respect for customer privacy, and partly to keep the list fresh.

Time-Life Libraries promotes a series concept in their sales approach. Their books, which are well written and heavily illustrated, are sold in sets. You have probably seen ads, for example, for their books about the planet Earth or the Old West. Customers are urged to try one book in the set, and if satisfied, can then purchase the rest when they are mailed to them on a regularly scheduled basis. The company does not generate enough income on the first book to make a profit and relies on customers' purchasing more than one book for an acceptable profit to be realized.

Time-Life has an extensive national print and broadcast advertising campaign. Magazine, newspaper, and direct-mail advertising contains descriptive information and coupons and telephone numbers for response. Broadcast advertising is used in two ways: (1) To support the print media coverage, with broadcast ads asking viewers to look in their Sunday newspapers or mailboxes for a Time-Life offer; or (2) to support direct sales ads that use an "800" number for response.

The telephone marketing centers try to coordinate their marketing efforts with a particular broadcast or print campaign. When customers are called, they are asked if they have seen the latest ad or received a brochure about a particular series of books. Customer recognition of the national advertising campaign aids in generating customer interest and sales.

Customer satisfaction is important. Time-Life wants to keep their customers for as long as possible. They know, as do all reputable direct marketers, that the key to obtaining and keeping customers starts with an honest, low-key sales approach.

The Script

The scripts used are straightforward, to the point, and delivered in a conversational, confident manner. The customer is first asked if he or she has received a brochure or seen an ad about a particular book. The book is then briefly described by the salesperson; the series concept and terms are explained, and the customer is asked to try the book on a ten-day trial. If the customer says yes, the address is verified and the terms are repeated.

Responses to common customer questions and objections are written in the script for the salespeople. Responses are designed to answer the question or meet the objection and then ask for the order (close).

Several procedures are used to reduce the number of orders that are returned. First of all, the customer is qualified several times. In the script, the customer is asked directly two or more times whether a purchase will be made if the book is satisfactory. Then, the next day, before the book is mailed to the customer, and so that the customer has had time to think about the book or talk it over with a spouse, the customer is called again to verify acceptance of the book on a trial basis. This verification step saves about 30 percent on returns.

The script is designed to include items that pique the interest of the customer and motivate the customer to read the book once it arrives. For example, the script is regionalized, if possible. A few facts about a local area are mentioned, as well as specific page numbers where the facts can be located in the book.

When the book arrives, the outer packaging instructs the customer to "open immediately." It is hoped that the customer will open the carton and, remembering the comments about the book, begin to thumb through it and decide to purchase it and the rest of the books in the series.

The salespeople work in four-hour shifts from 9 A.M. to 9 P.M. Monday through Friday, and from 9 A.M. to 5 P.M. on Saturdays. Each salesperson makes up to 150 calls in a four-hour shift, and averages three sales per hour. Salespeople are paid an hourly base rate and receive a commission for each customer who agrees to look at the book. Bonuses are given if the customer decides to buy the book and continue the series.

SAMPLE SCRIPT—
ABC TELEPHONE COMPANY PROMOTION

The ABC Telephone Company (a hypothetical company) manufactures and sells telephones for use in the home. They are in the middle of a promotional campaign to increase sales of their most popular model, the ABC Push-Tone Telephone. ABC has sent brochures to a list of potential customers. These brochures describe the ABC Push-Tone Telephone and its special end-of-year sale price.

The following script is used by salespeople who are calling the customers who received the mailing.

In addition to the script, the salespeople have familiarized themselves with the use of the telephone they are selling. They also have a copy of the brochure that was mailed (for reference), and a form on which to transcribe ordering information.

Hello, is this Mr./Ms. ———?

Mr./Ms.———, my name is ———. I'm calling for the ABC Telephone Company.

Did you receive the brochure we mailed to you, which described the special sale on our ABC Push-Tone Telephone?

(If answer is yes—go to B.)
(If answer is no—go to A).

(A) Well, I'd like to tell you a little bit about our sale. Would that be all right?

(If yes—go to C.)
(If no—go to "Objections" section.)

(B) Good. Then you've had a chance to learn about our telephone and its very special price. *(Go to C.)*

(C) Our ABC Push-Tone Telephone plugs into any telephone outlet and is approved by the Federal Communications Commission. The Push-Tone has several features not found on most telephones. For example, if you are calling a friend and get a busy signal, the telephone will remember the number you just dialed. When you are ready to call again, you just push *one* button and the telephone automatically redials the number *for* you. And not only will it remember the last number you dialed, but it will store up to *twelve* of your friends' numbers or important emergency numbers in the telephone's memory bank. By pushing one or two buttons, the telephone will *automatically* dial the number for you.

Best of all, instead of your having to make monthly rental payments on your present telephone, you will *own* your ABC phone. The special price of $———, which is 25 percent below our regular discount price, means that your new ABC telephone will pay for itself in *less* than a year.

And all parts and labor are guaranteed for a full year!

Now, Mr./Ms. ———, we have two payment plans. You can make one payment of ———, or three equal payments of ———. We can bill you, or you can use your credit card. Would you like us to bill you in one payment or in three equal payments, or would you like to charge this to your credit card?

(Take order information on order form.)

Now, Mr./Ms. ———, I'd like to verify your address for ordering purposes. Your address is ———? *(Repeat address.)*

(If credit card) Could you repeat your credit card number for me, please?

Thank you very much for your order. We will be shipping your ABC Push-Tone telephone at the special sale price of ——— within the next three working days. Your telephone should arrive in the next three to four weeks.

Thank you again for your order, Mr./Ms. ———. Good-bye.

RESPONSES TO SOME SAMPLE OBJECTIONS

Too expensive: It's really not as expensive as you might think, Mr./Ms. ———. For example, if you presently lease your telephone, you are paying rent of about $5 a month. At the end of one year you have actually paid $——— more in rent than the cost of the ABC Push-Tone Telephone! And, with the rental phone, you don't *own* it at the end of the year. You just have to keep *paying and paying.* At those rates, you can see that the Push-Tone is a real bargain.

Now, Mr./Ms. ———, would you like us to bill you in one payment or in three payments, or charge this to your credit card?

Don't have the money now: That's okay, Mr./Ms. ———, our payment plan breaks your payment into three equal payments of just $——— each, with no interest. And you don't have to make your first payment for thirty days.

Now, Mr./Ms. ———, would you like us to bill you on this easy payment plan, or would you like to charge this to your credit card?

I already own my own telephone: That's great, Mr./Ms. ———. Then you know how nice it is to own your own phone. As you know, it's getting close to Christmas. The ABC Push-Tone Telephone would make an excellent Christmas present. We can mail our telephone directly to you, or, if you like, we can deliver it to one of your friends specially gift-wrapped, complete with a Christmas card with your name embossed on the inside.

Now, Mr./Ms. ———, would you like us to deliver it to you, or would you like us to deliver it to a friend as a special present?

Have old wall outlet—no plug-in for telephone: That's not a problem, Mr./Ms. ———. For just $1, we will provide an adapter that fits onto your present telephone outlet so you can plug your new ABC Push-Tone Telephone right into the wall.

Now, would you like us to bill you in one payment or in three equal payments, or would you like to use your credit card?

COSTS

The most useful measurement tool in telephone selling is the cost-per-sale or cost-per-lead ratio. These ratios tell a marketer at a glance whether or not a promotion is producing satisfactory results. In addition, cost-per-lead and cost-per-sale ratios are primary measurement tools in other direct response media. This means that a common measuring denominator can be used to compare results from each of the media being tested. For example, when a cost per order of $4 in your telephone promotion is compared with a cost per sale of $9 in the print media, it is a good indication that the telephone may be the more favorable vehicle in which to roll out your promotion.

Mathematically, the determination of the cost ratio is simple; it is a simple division of the costs associated with your promotion by the number of orders or leads generated. The most difficult part of the process, just as it is in the other media, is the accurate capture of all costs associated with your promotion. When calculating costs, remember to include the following: operator costs, including salaries, incentives, and training; supervisory costs; overhead costs allocated to the promotion, including heat, light, rent, and so on; customer list costs; phone equipment charges and toll charges; creative costs, including script preparation and consultation costs.

It is important to remember that costs are a function of many variables that can skew your results one way or another. List costs, for example, can change from promotion to promotion. Your house list may be much less expensive than a list obtained from a list broker. The cost of maintaining a list with telephone numbers is expensive. Therefore your cost will be higher for the list containing telephone numbers. Many lists do not contain telephone numbers. You will more than likely need to hire a telephone number search service to look up those numbers for you. This is not inexpensive and can cost more than 15 or 20 cents per name, no matter whether a number was found for the name or not. If the number of names on your list that are not reachable by telephone is high, this will also increase your cost.

Operator Productivity and Compensation

The efficiency of your operators will also have an impact on costs. Your operators must be trained to dial numbers quickly and to terminate the call as soon as it is determined that the customer is not going to respond favorably to your message. Operators should also follow the script as closely as possible. A well-written script does wonders for efficient use of the telephone. Operators must be made to understand that in a large promotion even a few seconds saved overall can mean the difference between a successful promotion or a marginal one. The best way to convince your salespeople to make efficient and productive use of the telephone is to include incentives and bonuses for productivity in your wage structure. It is remarkable what compensation based on results can do to increase a salesperson's productivity level.

There is another reason to consider providing compensation based on productivity. Incentives and bonuses are costs that vary with levels of sales activity. Salaries and raises are essentially fixed costs once they are allocated, and do not automatically decrease when sales decrease. Payment based on performance puts you in a much more flexible situation to deal with changes in sales activity. When sales are down, your wage costs, which can be 60 to 70 percent of your promotion costs, will also decrease. Therefore your downside risk in any promotion is decreased.

Response Rates and Ratios

When compared on a cost-per-thousand basis to the direct response print or broadcast media, the telephone is relatively expensive. Per call costs can average from $2 to as much as $10 or more. But with the telephone you can expect to achieve a much higher number of sales per thousand than with the other media. In the print media, for example, a return of 2 to 3 percent is considered a success. The telephone, on the other hand, can have response rates up to ten times higher than that.

Generally, for residence customer calls, you can expect about 10 percent of your calls to result in a sale or lead. The ratio of sales to calls in the business marketplace can be more than twice as high. These are only ballpark estimates. This ratio can change quite dramatically, depending on the quality of your list, the promotion, the product or service, your target audience, and the skill of your sales team.

Of those factors, the list is usually the primary contributor to a high sales-to-call ratio. It doesn't matter how well conceived and polished your promotion is, how good your product is, or how skillful your salespeople are. Without a quality list that reaches the right people, your promotion is doomed from the start.

Another ratio you might find useful is cost as a percentage of sales. To determine this, first determine your estimated sales by multiplying your estimated number of orders times the average amount of sale per order (not cost per order). Then divide your total sales into your estimated promotion costs to find your cost-to-sales percentage (promotion costs/sales = % of cost to sales).

TESTING

The more experience you gain in the telephone marketing of your product, the better you will be at estimating results from future promotions. The best way to estimate potential response is to test. Test as many variables as you can—different offers, approaches, prices, and especially different lists of target audiences.

A testing tip that may save you time: Try to test first those lists that you feel will be the most successful. Your best list could be your house list or a list that contains the freshest names of your target market. The premise behind testing the list that has the highest potential for success is that if the tests with that list are unsuccessful, your tests on lower-quality lists will also be unsuccessful.

It is also relatively easy to test for response to a telephone-supported direct-mail campaign. To see if the telephone support was productive enough to justify a telephone roll-out to your full list, isolate a part of your list following a direct mailing and call those customers. Compare the results obtained from customers who received direct mail and a follow-up call with results obtained from the audience that received direct mail only.

STATUS OF TELEPHONE MARKETING REGULATION

As in any marketing effort, telephone marketing has legal and ethical parameters within which you should operate. Telephone marketers have so far been fortunate in the relative lack of restrictive legislation

106

that has been imposed on their industry. But the probability of restrictive legislation continues to exist, especially with the rapid growth of telephone marketing and the increasingly powerful voice of consumer action groups.

Up until the 1970s, very little federal or state legislative activity regarding telephone marketing had occurred. Then, the introduction of mechanized dialing and recording systems in the late 1970s prompted the federal government to study the need for regulation of the industry. Proposed legislation would have made it possible for those persons who did not wish to receive unsolicited telephone calls to have their names purged from lists used by telephone solicitors. After much debate and study the government decided that regulation on a federal level was not needed.

Regulatory activity is much greater on the state and local level. To date, more than fifty bills have been introduced in twenty-five states aimed at regulating "junk" calls. Several states consider telephone marketing to be door-to-door selling and have specified that telephone marketing be subject to the same laws as door-to-door selling. On a local level, various communities have passed ordinances designed to control certain telephone marketing activities. Before doing business in any state or community, it is advisable to take the precaution of becoming aware of and abiding by any restrictions that might apply to your telephone operations.

Operating Guidelines

Because the potential exists for increased legislation, two groups representing the telephone marketing industry, American Telephone and Telegraph Corporation and the Direct Mail Marketing Association, have made proposals for self-regulation within the industry. American Telephone and Telegraph Corporation has suggested setting limits on the duration of a selling call, the time of day it can be made, and the content of the call. The Direct Mail Marketing Association (DMMA) has created a set of guidelines that specifically relate to telephone marketing. These guidelines are voluntary, but the DMMA suggests that all telephone marketers follow them. The advantages to concurrence are increased customer satisfaction and a reduced likelihood that further legislation will be imposed. The guidelines are summarized here.

1. Fully disclose all offers clearly and honestly. Be prepared to substantiate any claims you make.
2. Disclose to your customers the name of the company you represent and the purpose of the call. You should not try to disguise your calls as surveys or research if in reality they are sales calls. Most customers can see

through this type of call. Your customers will be more appreciative of and more responsive to straightforwardness and honesty.

3. Fully disclose to the customer all product costs, guarantees, and terms.
4. Make telephone calls during reasonable hours (see section on calling times in this chapter).
5. Do not use automatic electronic dialing equipment unless the equipment automatically disconnects the call when the customer hangs up.
6. Never use high-pressure tactics.
7. Notify and obtain consent from the customer if you are recording the conversation and use a beeping device.
8. Remove contact names from your telephone list when requested. If at all possible, do not contact customers who have unlisted numbers unless permission has been given to do so.

In addition to these guidelines, laws and guidelines relating to direct marketing in general have been summarized in the Appendix. Use common sense in your telephone marketing promotions. Remember that you are interrupting an individual's daily routine with your solicitations. Honesty and courtesy to the customer are primary obligations of the direct marketer.

Summary of Important Points

The telephone can capture and hold the attention of your prospect. Its cost relative to a personal visit is low, and it can be more productive than a personal visit.

You can use the telephone in your business for one-step selling, to expand your market base, to develop leads, to eliminate cold calls, to contact marginal customers, to make and confirm appointments, to open new territories, to reestablish old accounts, to secure reorders, to convert trial customers into permanent customers, to up-sell and cross-sell, to support promotions in other media, and to provide service.

The script should be used in repetitive, noncomplex selling situations. Scripted selling is highly structured and depends upon a well-written script that directs and anticipates most consumer response.

Unscripted selling is more personalized and is used when selling complex, technical, high-priced, low-volume items.

Even when not using a script, you should be thoroughly prepared to answer questions, overcome objections, and listen and respond to customer comments.

Prerecorded selling (ADRMP) is a high-volume, consistent way to deliver a sales message but has a tendency to irritate the customer if not handled correctly.

Calling at the proper time is a combination of courtesy, common sense, and knowledge of the target market.

Effective telephone sales personnel have acquired mastery of verbal sales techniques.

Outside services can be useful when quick lead times are required and when promotions are repetitive, high volume, and not too technical.

Cost per sale and cost per lead are useful and universal measurement ratios.

Operator productivity can be influenced by compensation based on performance.

Although per call costs can be expensive relative to costs in other media, response rates from telephone promotions can be much higher.

The legal and ethical guidelines of EDM are based on honesty and common courtesy.

8

CABLE
TELEVISION

HISTORY

Cable television was invented in 1948, just one year after the networks began broadcasting programs nationally. John Walson, a TV salesman in receptionless Mahanoy City, Pennsylvania, built a mountaintop antenna and ran a cable back to his store. Along the cable's path he wired neighborhood homes, thereby creating the first community antenna television system (CATV). Since that time, and especially in recent years, CATV has been growing at a phenomenal pace. Today there are more than 4200 CATV systems in the United States, with more than 30 million subscribers, or 30 percent of all United States television households, double that of six years before. New subscribers are being added at the rate of more than 250,000 a month. Some industry experts estimate that by 1990, almost 60 percent of all television households will have cable.

Still, it has taken more than thirty years for cable to begin to catch on at this rate. There are two main reasons for this.

First, cable was perceived until recently as just a means to enhance a TV picture in areas where broadcast signals were blocked by buildings, mountains, or sheer distance. So at first cable systems

110

sprang up only in rural areas where viewers were the most eager to subscribe to the systems.

Second, the federal government restricted the development of cable TV to protect local broadcast stations from competitive broadcasts from larger stations being carried into a local territory by cable. The Federal Communications Commission in the 1970s loosened those regulations, allowing cable and its programs virtually unrestricted movement.

Today cable is taking root in big cities, and cable companies frantically vie for the franchise rights to unwired cities. As competition heats up for lucrative territories, the bidding becomes intense.

The financial part of cable contracts with the cities is similar. Most cities get 3 to 5 percent of a cable company's gross, and contracts run for fifteen years.

Other methods are used by cable companies to persuade cities to choose them as cable service suppliers. Cable companies have been known to take out full-page ads and in some cases persuade influential local residents to join their payrolls. And extravagant services are offered. For example, Warner-Amex recently made a bid to Dallas that included a system containing 104 channels. Most contracts now include clauses requiring that the new systems have the technological capability for eventual two-way computerized television.

Even with the competition for cable so intense and growth so rapid, many large cities, including Denver, Chicago, Boston, Fort Worth, and several parts of New York City are just beginning to be wired.

REASONS FOR GROWTH

Why is cable growing so quickly? Anyone who subscribes to a cable system will tell you that cable can offer more channels than regular broadcast television, and there is greater variety. In addition to local stations, cable systems offer stations from other cities, such as WTBS in Atlanta, WOR in New York, or WGN in Chicago, as well as channels created specifically for cable, such as ESPN (sports), CNN (news), MTV (music), Nickelodeon (children's programming), CHN (health), and, at extra cost, Home Box Office, The Movie Channel, Escapade, Cinemax, and Showtime (commercial-free movies and entertainment).

The availability of a multitude of commercial-free channels and channels containing alternative programming is having a profound effect on traditional network television; the "big three" networks are undergoing a decline in viewership unprecedented in the history of broadcast television. With cable, videodiscs, and home video recorders offering viewers more variety and convenience, viewers are turning away from network TV for the first time since TV began.

The Nielson ratings showed that near the end of 1982, the networks were averaging about 83 percent of the entire TV audience, certainly a significant amount. But just two years before, the figure was 91 percent.

At the time of this writing a ratings sample showed that the overall prime time ratings were at their lowest in two years. Although CBS "won" the sample week, its overall rating for the week was 12.8, which meant that, in an average minute during the week, only 12.8 percent of the nation's homes with TV were tuned to CBS.

Cable is one of the primary reasons for this loss in network viewership. Cable industry experts now optimistically estimate that by 1985, the network share will be down to 67 percent. A recent study by Nielson has found that cable homes spend as much as one third of their viewing time watching nonnetwork TV. Most of this viewing time goes to independent stations.

The fact that more and more viewers are turning to cable is not going unnoticed by network broadcasters. They are more than a little concerned that their virtual monopoly of the viewing public and their control over what the public will see and when they will watch is coming to an end. They are looking for ways to deal with this threat.

In an attempt to stay abreast of the changes taking place in the industry, the networks or their subsidiaries all control or have partial interests in cable systems or channels.

OPPORTUNITIES FOR DIRECT MARKETERS

The rapid growth of cable is creating new opportunities for advertisers. International Resource Development, Inc., an advertising research firm, predicts that by 1990, 100 cable networks out of a total of 141 will be advertising-supported, with advertising revenues of $1.6 billion.

Advertising results so far indicate that direct response marketing is the key to making the best use of cable TV as an advertising medium. Because there are so many cable systems and channels available, it is extremely difficult for advertisers to make certain a sales message will be viewed. A report issued at the 1982 National Cable Television Association's (NCTA) annual convention showed that consumers do not yet place a great value on cable's ability to deliver dozens of channels. Instead, they are only concerned about getting four or five special channels featuring programming such as movies and sports. More significantly, the cable industry lacks the audience measurement tools that broadcast networks have, such as the Nielson and Arbitron ratings. Leonard Matthews, president of the American Association of Advertising Agencies, says that although cable is beginning to attract commercial advertisers, the industry may never reach its potential until it can develop methods to measure audiences and prove performance. A number of audience measurement tests are now underway, including one completed by the Research Standards Committee and the NCTA, which will test different ways of measuring TV audiences on cable.

Until definitive measurement techniques are developed for cable, commercial advertisers will continue to be reluctant to take the plunge into cable. Those advertisers who are using cable are attempting to overcome the uncertainty of message delivery by segmenting their audiences and targeting particular programs.

Direct-Marketing Potential

Direct marketers, however, are finding that the measurement tools inherent in their technique provide them with enough data to prove that advertising on cable can be done very successfully. In fact, cable channels are using results from EDM promotions to prove their levels of audience penetration. For example, Ted Turner's WTBS in Atlanta, a station that transmits its programs by satellite to cable systems all over the United States, was having a great deal of trouble attracting commercial advertisers willing to pay rates relative to WTBS's claimed audience penetration. To establish their audience coverage, WTBS encouraged the use of EDM promotions, even setting up their own "800" number response and order processing center. By taking orders from these promotions on a per inquiry basis (that is, the station received a percentage of the money received for each order), WTBS was able to get credit for their coverage and, at the same time, by using the "800" number for response, to establish their coverage much faster than could Arbitron or Nielson.

How to Use Cable

How can direct marketers use cable? First of all, most cable channels, except for the superstations from Atlanta, Chicago, and New York, have narrow program formats: all news, sports, and so on. No matter where you are positioned in a program or block of time, the audience you will be reaching will have similar characteristics. Because of this "narrowcasting," cable audiences offer marketers a rifleshot effect rather than the shotgun effect achieved in ROS or network advertising. An EDM promotion using a product or service oriented toward the audience on a cable channel will therefore produce higher sales volumes with fewer people. In effect, cable TV narrowcasting can be considered to be more like the print media or radio than broadcasting. If you know what type of audience you are trying to reach, there is a large amount of demographic information available about subscribers, and you can use this information to key your product and promotion to those subscribers.

Most cable audiences, for example, tend to have higher per capita incomes than noncable subscribers in the same areas, especially in new cable areas. This is because when a cable company starts to wire a city for cable, they tend to wire first within their franchises those homes that can most easily afford it. As cable matures, the audience income mix of cable subscribers will begin to more closely correspond to that of noncable audiences.

Another important statistic: Cable TV homes watch an average of 1.3 more hours of television per day than noncable homes.

PURCHASING TIME

There are two basic ways for direct marketers to purchase time on cable. First of all, spots can be purchased from local cable systems to be televised within that system's area. The National Cable Television Association reports that only about 15 percent of the cable systems in the United States sell advertising time, but that number is growing.

Secondly, spots can be purchased from one of the cable network program suppliers that transmit their signals by satellite to local cable systems.

Satellite Systems

The procedure involved in the transmission of programs by these networks is rather simple to understand. Unlike traditional stations that broadcast signals directly into the home, the cable networks beam their signal to an orbiting communications satellite. The signal is sent back to cable systems that have receiving discs. From the disc the cable operators can then distribute the programming to their subscribers via coaxial cable. The independent stations of WTBS, WOR, and WGN are called superstations because, unlike other independent stations, superstations transmit their signals to cable systems all over the United States. In effect, the purchase of a spot on a superstation is similar to purchasing a national network spot. Today WTBS has a 22 percent level of penetration throughout the country, while WGN and WOR stand at 13 and 6 percent. And although each of these superstation's coverage is most concentrated in markets closest to the city of origination, coverage outside of these areas is becoming more significant as more cable systems are signed up.

114

Spot Costs

This type of coverage—not only by the superstations that have programming typical of independent stations, with a mixture of movies, local sports, reruns of syndicated programs, and news and talk shows, but also by the narrowcasting of other cable network channels—is an advantage to the direct response marketer. The cost of spots on these stations is considerably less on a per viewer basis than on network and noncable stations, a cost difference caused in part by the lack of an accurate audience measurement system and the reluctance of general advertisers to use this coverage. The ESPN sports network, for example, reaches more than 5 million homes through over 700 systems. A two-minute spot costs about $900.

This lower cost and the lack of general advertising mean that direct marketers will have more opportunities to position their advertising and can do this at a cost lower than typical run-of-station rates on noncable channels. This lower cost per viewer also translates into a lower cost per product order, and may mean the difference between a successful promotion on cable or a mediocre one on noncable alternatives.

Cable Advertising Contacts

The National Cable Television Association publishes the *Cable Advertising Directory*, which lists cable systems that carry advertising. To obtain a copy, which costs $10, contact the NCTA at 918 16th Street N.W.; Washington, D.C. 20006.

There are also a growing number of companies that represent cable systems and networks. However, if you have determined the markets you are trying to reach in your promotion, it may be to your advantage to find out if there are cable systems in those markets and contact the cable managers personally. You may be able to negotiate a better rate or position for your ads.

Many of the advertising-supported cable networks, including ESPN, USA, and the superstations, have in-house sales forces and can be contacted directly for time purchases.

A typical promotion schedule may include initial purchases of time on one or several of the cable networks to ensure national exposure. By monitoring phone or mail response from these buys, it can then be determined in which markets response was greatest. Spot purchases can then be made on the cable systems serving those markets.

HOME SHOPPING

The public's attitude toward the commercial message is beginning to change. The cable medium, just like the print medium, is now giving the viewer the chance to control viewing habits. With cable, as with videocassette recorders and videodiscs, viewers can watch a program that is repeated several times a month. The viewer can choose to watch a part of or all of a program just as a person may read a magazine article and put the magazine down for later reading.

Of more significance to the marketer or advertiser is the influence of the commercial-free cable channels. When confronted with irritating or annoying advertising, viewers do not find it difficult to make the simple switch to a commercial-free channel.

Commercial-free competition is causing advertisers and advertising-supported stations to rethink their advertising strategies. Some independent TV stations, for example, realizing that they are now competing against commercial-free and advertising-supported cable channels, have rescheduled their commercial messages so that movies and special programs are only interrupted two or three times for messages instead of the traditional six or more times in a two-hour program. In many European countries commercials are only allowed during certain blocks of time in the viewing day, and virtually never within a program. Perhaps the pressure caused by viewers opting for commercial-free channels will motivate advertising-supported channels to rethink their commercial scheduling and arrive at a system closer to that of the Europeans.

The length and format of the commercial may also undergo some change. Marketers and advertisers are beginning to realize that in order to sell products in the face of commercial-free competition, the way in which the sales message is presented may have to change. The sales message must be presented in such a way that the viewer will *want* to stay with the channel or, as far-fetched as it may seem, turn *to* the channel to view the sales message.

Several experiments are now underway on various cable channels that are testing alternatives to traditional advertising. One of the cable industry's futuristic ideas has always been shopping via cable. The viewer would turn on the TV, flip to the retailing channel, examine the goods displayed there, place an order through a control box connected to the TV and to a computer at the transmission facilities, and sit back and wait for delivery. Of course, television EDM is essentially home shopping; products are displayed on the TV and ordered by phone or mail. But it has only been recently that entire programs or entire channels have been devoted to a shop-at-home format. And only recently has there been the technology available for computerized two-way TV.

Instead of traditional thirty- to 120-second advertising, marketers are using blocks of thirty to sixty minutes to tell their sales stories. They are finding that the extra length of the message gives advertisers a better opportunity to demonstrate products and the viewers a better opportunity to find out about products.

116

How do you keep viewers' attention through a thirty- to sixty-minute commercial? Basically, marketers are finding that viewers will watch and respond to those lengthy messages if those messages contain useful information about products of interest to the viewer.

The following examples illustrate some of the testing that is going on in this field. These examples are trials that utilize the telephone or mail for response. In the next chapter we will discuss and present examples of testing in the field of computer-assisted and two-way interactive television.

Catalog Shows

"The Sharper Image Living Catalog" and "Video Mail Order" are two direct response television programs that offer products in a catalog format.

"The Sharper Image Living Catalog" is a cable TV version of "The Sharper Image" print catalog. "The Sharper Image" claims to offer the world's most unusual products. The program is a half hour in length. Each product is displayed and demonstrated for one to two minutes by the magazine's publisher or his assistant. The products can be ordered through a toll-free "800" number.

"Video Mail Order" began operation in the first quarter of 1983. Products offered for sale on the program are obtained from up to fifty different catalog companies, each providing five products with an average retail price of $75. The programming runs twenty-four hours and is presented in continuous five-hour loops. Viewers can order products through toll-free numbers. Orders are processed at a response center and forwarded to merchandisers for fulfillment.

"The Home Shopping Show"

"The Home Shopping Show" is a half-hour program in a talk show format. Each show is split into three nine-minute segments. Advertisers can purchase one, two, or all three of these segments. Two hosts interview representatives of the advertisers. These representatives dispense information and advice about their products and give demonstrations. The sales messages are usually low-key and interesting. For example, Grolier Enterprises provided a children's book author to discuss the importance of reading for children and to offer memberships in their Disney Book Club. Pillsbury Company bought a special half-hour program to promote its bake-off contest. They offered viewers free coupons, free recipes, and a recipe book for $1. American Products demonstrated a rotary airless paint sprayer and offered it for sale through a toll-free number at a $30 discount.

"The Shopping Game"

"The Shopping Game" is a cable program with a format similar to a daytime TV game show. Participants have an opportunity to win products based on successful responses to questions from the game show host. As each product is won, a direct response commercial, usually 30 to 120 seconds in length, explains the product. Each commercial contains a toll-free number that viewers can call to order the same products the participants have won. Examples of products range from a $6.99 record album to a $341 trip to Mexico. The program is owned by Holder-Kennedy, a Nashville firm. The firm uses its own operators rather than an independent telephone response service to take orders generated from its programs.

Cableshop

The J. Walter Thompson Advertising Agency and the Adams-Russell cable system are combining efforts to present a new advertising service called Cableshop to viewers in Peabody, Massachusetts. The service is based on the premise that viewers will voluntarily turn to advertising for products and services that they are interested in buying. With this service, viewers can use a toll-free telephone line to request commercial programming in addition to scheduled advertising. The service uses four channels of a fifty-two-channel system. One channel is used for displaying the directory of what is scheduled to be shown on the other three channels. Most of the commercials, or "infomercials," as these longer cable commercials are sometimes called, are three to seven minutes in length. The advertised products can be ordered through a special direct response telephone number. Initial charter advertisers include twenty national advertisers and a small group of Boston area retailers. The test began in March 1982, and lasted nine months. Results of the test were made available to advertising subscribers in 1983.

Summary of Important Points

The measurement tools inherent in EDM are allowing direct marketers the opportunity to profit from the explosive growth of the cable television industry.

Cable time purchases are relatively inexpensive, and the procedures are in many cases similar to those for purchasing national network spots.

The proliferation of experiments in home shopping and the use of longer commercial formats (infomercials) mean additional sales opportunities for direct marketers.

9

THE NEW
TECHNOLOGIES

VIEWDATA

Several electronic information systems utilizing centralized computer-maintained data bases are now being tested in various parts of the world. Most of these systems include advertising and home shopping services in addition to other information services ranging from news or sports information to movie listings. The information is transmitted directly to the home via cable or telephone lines for reception on a home computer or television set. The viewer can call up information at will from the data base located at the transmission facilities. In many systems the consumer can communicate directly with the computer via a special keyboard attached to the TV. Information can be retrieved, products can be ordered and processed, or responses such as opinions to a political poll can be electronically recorded by the computer. This interactive two-way process is called Viewdata.

Interactive Television Defined

Because the concept is so new, the terminology for interactive television is sometimes misunderstood. Some marketers refer to interactive TV as telemarketing, a term that to many means selling by telephone. Others define interactive TV as the combination of selling through TV and purchasing by telephone and mail. This book will assume interactive or two-way TV to be the same as that of television EDM, where the response to the electronic TV promotion can be independent of the transmission line.

Viewdata Defined and Described

Viewdata will be defined as any system with a direct link between the transmission of a data signal and the reception of a viewer response, where transmission and response are accomplished via a single phone or cable line, and where the data base can be accessed and manipulated by that viewer activity. Viewdata will therefore be considered as a part of the spectrum of television EDM, where response mechanisms such as the telephone and mail can be separate from the transmission of the signal.

Viewdata systems operate similarly to the print media. Data is retrieved a page at a time, as one might turn the pages of a newspaper or magazine. The electronic data base, however, can be continually updated. New "pages" can be added or deleted, or prices of products can be changed, all without affecting the rest of the data base. In the print media, such revisions might mean the need for a reissuance of a new catalog or magazine.

Although Viewdata is still in its infancy, it represents some exciting possibilities for consumers and marketers. With Viewdata, a consumer is free to access a data base that can contain thousands of pages of information and display selected information on a screen, all within seconds. Depending on the system and the size of the data base, users can get up-to-the-minute stock market information, read the latest news as it comes from the wire services and before it is in the newspapers, make plane reservations, read a book review, mail an electronic letter, find a new recipe for dinner, or receive any of a myriad of other information-related services.

With Viewdata, the consumer takes an active part in the marketing process. Various home shopping services are available, their data bases containing thousands of products that can be purchased. If a consumer were interested in cameras, for example, he or she could ask the computer to provide a list of all cameras in the data base that were of a specific type, such as 35 millimeter, or in a specific price range. The consumer could then compare each of the cameras on the list and their descriptions to determine the camera best suited for himself or herself. If he or she decides to make a purchase, the consumer inputs some basic purchase information, including a credit card number or other information to indicate how the purchase will be made. The computer then records the information and sets up procedures for delivery of the camera to the consumer. All this is accomplished without leaving the livingroom easychair.

For marketers, interactive capability represents a new way to reach consumers. But because the viewer plays an active role in the process of selecting and purchasing products and services, the strategies used to get the consumer to consider a marketer's products will also change. Because the control rests with the viewer, and because it is still difficult to "glamourize" a data base, the marketer will need to become more of an information provider and less of an impression maker; information is what the consumer will be asking for in order to make a decision.

VIEWDATA SYSTEMS

Prestel

Prestel was the first large-scale interactive computer-based information service. It was developed and is controlled by the British Postal and Telegraph service. It was begun with 1,500 subscribers and now has more than 12,000, predominantly businesses. More than 250 information providers supply the data base, which contains over 250,000 pages of information, including news, business information, travel information, advertising, an encyclopedia, stock market information, games, and restaurant guides. Subscribers can select this information from the data base by using a special keypad attached to their television sets. The viewer pays anywhere from zero cents per frame for advertising to up to ten cents per frame for other types of information.

The first demographic audience data on two-way TV were recently compiled by Prestel, and the results have just been made available to the public. Although the study concerns British consumers, the results can be assumed to resemble the responses of Americans, since the life styles and habits of the British and American people are similar.

Excerpts from the study show that the majority of the subscribers would do more home shopping and would participate more heavily in direct response offers if the direct marketing activities of advertisers were expanded. Although response to offers of leaflets and brochures was high, at 87 percent for residential users and 59 percent for business users, the percentage of those who actually buy goods and services was much lower; 40 percent of the residential users and only 8 percent of the business customers reported buying goods and services through the direct response offers.

The study also breaks down goods and services orders by product categories and by categories of business customers and residential customers. For example, among products purchased through EDM, electronic goods were the most popular. They were purchased by 13 percent of the business locations and 23 percent of the residential locations.

More detailed information about the Prestel study can be obtained by writing to Gary H. Arlen, Arlen Communications, Inc., P.O. Box 40871, Washington, D.C., 20016.

Antiope

The French Post and Telegraph Office has developed a Viewdata system they call Antiope. They have begun a vigorous campaign to replace all of their telephone directories by installing Antiope terminals free in 30 million French households by 1990. Telephone numbers and addresses will be accessed from the Antiope data base. Cost of installation of the system will be offset by the cost of producing, distributing, and revising printed directories.

The French system is somewhat like the British Prestel, although the Antiope system has better resolution and graphics. It also is compatible with most software systems and any type of terminal.

Other International Viewdata Systems

Germany, Switzerland, Australia, Italy, and Canada are among those experimenting with Viewdata systems. Germany, for example, is operating a system they call Bildschirmtext. Its 40,000 users have access via their terminals to, among other information categories, a data base of products from more than twenty catalogs of goods and services.

Canada is experimenting with a system they call Teledon. Terminals were installed in hundreds of homes in Manitoba, Calgary, and Vancouver, British Columbia. Users have access to a data base that contains farm information, news, product information, stock prices, and advertising. In addition to basic text and graphics, the Teledon system also uses a form of animation.

Viewtron and Sceptre

Viewtron is a joint venture by Viewdata Corporation, a subsidiary of Knight-Ridder newspapers, and AT&T. It is a data retrieval service that gives subscribers the opportunity to access a data base that contains more than 18,000 pages of information. The data base is provided by, among others, Knight-Ridder, *The New York Times*, Dow-Jones, and CBS Publications.

Information is accessed via a special videotex terminal called Sceptre. The microprocessor-based terminal incorporates advanced features with a self-contained high-speed communications link that turns an ordinary television set and a telephone line into a system for accessing the videotex data base.

A wide variety of information is available, including travel information, educational instruction, and various products for sale. Advertisers include JCPenney, Sears, Eastern Airlines, and Merrill, Lynch, Pierce, Fenner, and Smith.

QUBE

QUBE is a Viewdata service developed and operated by Warner-Amex, Inc. First launched in Columbus, Ohio, in 1977, QUBE has now expanded to Cincinnati, and additional QUBE systems are scheduled for Chicago, Dallas, Pittsburgh, Houston, and St. Louis. The QUBE system in Ohio is currently linked to more than 30,000 homes.

QUBE uses cable to link a home TV with a central computer. Subscribers use a calculatorlike device that allows them to respond to questions, choose alternative programs, vote their opinions on issues, or order products advertised on the screen. By using the computer to select only certain subscribers, QUBE can target programs to specific audiences, just as a direct marketer might use a mailing list to reach a specific target audience.

So far the home shopping portion of QUBE has not been profitable for marketers. The *Wall Street Journal* (10/81) reported that there was much disappointment and little usage of the interactive capabilities of the system. More recently, a spokesperson for Warner-Amex ("On the Horizon," 1982) agreed that research is still scarce on the sales impact of QUBE, but contended that the potential exists for systems of this type to be the "store of the future."

The Shopping Channel

Times Mirror Satellite Co. and Comp-U-Card of America, Inc., a discount buying service, are offering a service called The Shopping Channel. A viewer uses a keyboard to request information about products. The system selects products that meet the viewer's specifications and displays them on a TV screen. Products can be either examined or purchased. If the decision is made to purchase, the computer completes the transaction and arranges for shipment of the product to a viewer-designated destination.

More than 50,000 homes are currently equipped with The Shopping Channel. Subscribers to the system pay a monthly membership fee to Comp-U-Card.

TELETEXT

Teletext is a generic term for one-way broadcasting of text information to a TV set. A loop of several hundred pages of information is broadcast frame by frame (page by page) at a very high speed. The viewer uses a special adapter and keypad to select and display a page from the loop. Teletext can transmit words and color graphics onto a TV screen by means of an unused portion of the regular TV broadcast signal. Teletext is used to transmit news, weather, announcements, and stock market information.

Teletext systems are a part of the movement toward electronic journalism; many newspapers, TV stations, and other media are experimenting with Teletext as a way of printing news and other information on video screens and then broadcasting those screens full of information to viewers through their TV sets.

Teletext and Viewdata Differences

Teletext differs from Viewdata in that the information provided by Teletext is broadcast without the need for cable or telephone lines. The drawback is that Teletext is a *one-way system*; viewers are restricted to the data being transmitted by the systems' operators, which is considerably less data than that available through Viewdata systems. Also, viewer response to any advertising promotion must be independent of the system.

Examples of Some Teletext Systems

One example of Teletext is the transmission of simultaneous close-captioned dialogue by network broadcasters. The printed dialogue is run on the bottom of the TV screen to help the hearing impaired understand and enjoy network programs.

In Kentucky, the U. S. Department of Agriculture is sponsoring a test called Project Green Thumb. Two hundred farmers are connected to a Teletext system that provides them with access to local weather maps, soil conditions, commodity prices, and other farm-related information.

In England, Teletext systems include the BBC's Ceefax and the IBA's Oracle.

KIRO Teletext

KIRO TV, a network affiliate of CBS in Seattle, Washington, has announced that it has begun operation of a Teletext system. The 800 pages of information include maps of the city's freeways showing where traffic is congested, ferry schedules containing last-minute changes, the latest sports scores, news headlines, stock reports, film reviews, weather reports, and school lunch menus. CBS provides up to 100 pages of national and world news.

To gain access to this information, viewers must purchase an adapter and remote control box ($35 to $40). Eventually, TV sets will be built so that no special equipment will be necessary. RCA has promised to begin constructing TV sets with built-in adapters as soon as the FCC approves one standardized type of adaptation system.

To make the system profitable for the station, KIRO includes advertising that appears on the screen with the information. A viewer wishing to see a sports score may see an ad for a sporting goods store at the bottom of the page, for example. Because this system is one-way, like all Teletext systems, customer response to direct response advertising must be by telephone or through the mail.

Teletext systems, like Viewdata systems, can only transmit printed words and graphic illustrations, such as maps or designs; they cannot transmit sound. Future enhancements to Teletext and Viewdata systems include the ability to transmit pictures and sound.

VIDEODISCS

Although the technology is much more complex than the following definition, a videodisc is essentially film on a record. Prerecorded movies, educational programs, athletic events, concerts, and other information can be stored in thousands of pictures within the microscopic grooves of each disc. Each disc can hold more than 50,000 individual pictures. The discs are played almost as you might play a record album, except that a special videodisc player is required, the disc spins at nearly 2,000 RPM, and the conventional needle is replaced by a laser. The video can be played through a television set, and the audio can be directed through stereo speakers. Video and audio quality is superior to film or videotape.

The freeze-frame feature found on some videodisc systems is of great interest to direct marketers. A user can select an individual numbered frame and freeze it on the video monitor. Art collections, books, even encyclopedias can be retrieved by the viewer one frame at a time. The significance of this feature to the direct marketer is the potential to store an entire catalog of products on a single disc. The disc can then be used just as one would turn the pages of a catalog.

The videodisc also lets the user see a product in action; a marketer could provide on the same disc a shop-at-home program, informational commercial messages, or demonstrations of some of the products in the catalog.

Sears is one of several companies that has been experimenting with the videodisc as a direct marketing tool. Sears transferred their entire 1981 summer catalog onto a videodisc manufactured by Pioneer, and delivered it without charge to a sample audience of Pioneer LaserDisc owners. Because of its freeze frame capability, the Pioneer system allowed the user to search the "catalog" frame by frame (page by page). The user could also move to another area of the disc and see selected products in short informational commercials. Products could be purchased by ordering over the telephone or by visiting a local Sears store.

The ability to access actual pictures (photographs) and to further see products in actual use with audio are advantages that the videodisc system offers over viewdata-type interaction systems. Viewdata has no audio, is limited to displays of text or graphics, and has limited animation capability.

It is too early yet to know whether the distribution of videodisc catalogs to videodisc users will be a profitable venture. Although the transferring of catalogs to a videodisc is cost effective when compared with the printing and other costs associated with the production of regular catalogs, success is really dependent upon the future number of videodisc owners. Because there are relatively few units in use nationwide, the introduction of catalog service on a regular basis may be some time in coming. In addition, there are several manufacturers and distributors of videodisc systems. These systems are all noncompatible with each other. That is, a videodisc manufactured by Pioneer will not play on any other videodisc system. RCA's videodisc system, for example, uses a needle instead of a laser to play its disc. The RCA system also does not have the freeze frame feature, making the system incompatible with a catalog format.

There are indications that the videodisc market is not as strong as originally forecasted. Although video and audio quality is superb, the major drawback of these systems appears to be their inability to record programs off the air. Consumers seem to be opting in ever increasing numbers for videocassette recorders, which do have off-the-air recording ability but less video and audio quality.

Sears may still find a use for the videodisc system, even if the user-owner market remains weak. One alternative they are considering is placing the systems in their catalog stores and making the system interactive with computers at Sears headquarters.

VIDEOCASSETTE RECORDERS

Videocassette recorders (VCRs) are rapidly gaining widespread acceptance among consumers. Since 1975, when Sony introduced the first VCR, sales of home VCRs have been growing almost geometrically. An April 26, 1982, article in *Newsweek* predicts that by 1990, more than 40 million VCRs will be in regular use, the majority of them in the home.

One of the main reasons for the popularity of the VCR is that it gives the viewer the option of being able to prerecord a program and then watch that program at a more convenient time. This freedom to watch a program at a time chosen by the viewer, rather than the one-time only format dictated by the network broadcasters, in a sense returns control to the viewer. This control gives television the flexibility of the print medium: The viewer can watch (read) as much or as little of a program as desired, just as he or she may pick up a magazine, read an article or two, and set it down for later reading.

Probably the most common use of the VCR as a direct sales tool today is in the sale of products business-to-business and in the selling of high-ticket items by a salesperson to a consumer. The video presentation acts as a sales aid to the personal presentation. Usually a sales message has been prerecorded on videotape, perhaps by the president of the company or an actor. The assistance provided by the videotape helps the salesperson to get the sales message to the client in a persuasive and effective way.

VCR Direct-Marketing Opportunitites

The rapid growth and penetration of this new electronic medium into the home represents a staggering potential for the direct marketer. Up to now, however, marketers have not made significant attempts to use the VCR as a direct marketing medium, and for several good reasons.

Most important, the freedom of being able to watch a prerecorded program when one pleases also means that the viewer can choose to watch that program free of any commercial messages. Many viewers will simply edit them out of a program that they have recorded. It is obvious that consumer reluctance to view commercial messages within prerecorded programs makes it nearly impossible for a marketer to sell goods and services within those programs. It is probably not very likely that consumer attitudes will change to the point where commercial presentations will be appreciated on cassettes that contain entertainment programming.

Marketers may, however, find some success in providing nonentertainment prerecorded programs to consumers in a format similar to the shop-at-home programs on cable television. As of yet it is still not as cost effective to distribute tapes to consumers in the same way a direct marketer now distributes printed catalogs. Production costs can be high and the videotapes themselves are expensive. These high costs make it absolutely necessary that a marketer be able to reach the exact audience he or she has targeted for his or her products. Misses can be expensive.

Marketers may find some success distributing video catalogs containing prestigious, high-margin products. The uniqueness of this marketing approach may yield profitable results.

VCR Limitations

Currently only top-of-the-line VCRs have limited freeze frame capability, a feature that is a necessity if a marketer wants to be able to present detailed information or a large number of products within a video catalog. The freeze frame feature on VCRs is not as precise as that of the videodisc systems such as Pioneer's LaserDisc, where it is possible to select and freeze a specific prenumbered frame, just as a consumer would turn to a specific page in a catalog.

Another drawback in the potential of the VCR is that VCRs use two different videotape formats, BETA and VHS. A BETA videotape will not play in a VHS machine, and vice versa. A BETA tape, however, will play in any BETA machine and VHS tapes will play in any VHS machine, regardless of the manufacturer. A direct marketer considering the distribution of videotapes to consumers must be able to identify those consumers with BETA machines and those with VHS, a potentially difficult task.

As more and more consumers acquire VCRs and make use of them as one of their primary entertainment and educational sources, direct marketers will have no choice but to begin to experiment with the videotape as one of their direct marketing tools. But until ways can be found to make large-scale use of this medium cost effective, direct marketers will have to concentrate on other approaches to getting their electronic messages to the consumer.

DIGITAL BROADCASTING

It is now possible to transmit (mail) a piece of information using radio frequencies to a terminal where the message can be read and responded to. The information is received by a special decoder attached to a computer or a line printer.

Digital Broadcasting Corporation experimented with Digital

Broadcasting several years ago. The experiment was designed to assess the feasibility of transmitting messages from a minicomputer to FM receivers attached to line printers at several locations.

More recently, National Public Radio and National Public Utilities Corporation announced that they have formed a joint venture called INC Telecommunications that will deliver software programs digitally by satellite to 220 public radio stations. For $40 a month the programs can be received by any subscriber owning a personal computer. A special decoder is attached to the computer that translates the FM signal for the user.

Digital Broadcasting is essentially a one-way noninteractive system. Because the signal is broadcast over FM, subscribers can only receive the digital signals and cannot transmit back to the host computer as is possible with Viewdata, or with a microcomputer connected to a data base via telephone line.

MICROCOMPUTERS

Microcomputers, also called personal or home computers, may hold some promise for direct marketers. Through the use of a modem (telephone coupler) the computer can be connected by telephone line to any number of selected data bases around the country. There are companies that will provide access to a multitude of informational data bases and provide a number of communications services as well. One such company is The Source, a subsidiary of The Reader's Digest Association, Inc. For a one-time charge and a fee based on usage, The Source will provide access to more than 1200 programs and services. Examples include the UPI news service, an electronic travel service, The New York Times consumer library, the latest stock information, electronic games, general entertainment, educational programs, an executive reading service, financial services, additional computer programming power, and data base storage. More important for the direct marketer, there are also marketing and mailing services available. "Chat" lets one computer user "talk" with any other subscriber who is on-line at the same time. "Talking" is accomplished by typing and receiving messages.

An electronic mail service is available. This service lets you transmit to other subscribers simple messages or lengthy reports quickly and economically.

Subscribers also have access to an electronic department store called Comp-U-Star. The Comp-U-Star data base contains more than 30,000 items. You can quickly comparison shop by product, manufacturer, model number, product characteristics, or price. Any of the products can be ordered on-line by keying in requested billing information.

It may be a few years before it becomes profitable to market products and services by computer. But the medium is growing rapidly. Some estimates suggest that as many as 7 million homes will be equipped with home computers by 1984. However, a much smaller number than that will have subscribed to a data base service such as The Source.

Microcomputers are expensive, and many models are out of the price range of most families. But as technology improves and prices drop, it may not be long before the microcomputer becomes commonplace (if not a necessity) in almost every home.

ELECTRONIC MAIL

As mailing costs continue to rise, it is not surprising that alternatives to traditional mail are becoming more popular. The telephone, for example, is increasingly being utilized as an alternative to mail. The use of the "800" number for business transactions, reservations, orders, and electronic funds transfer are becoming commonplace.

More and more private companies are offering to deliver "mail" faster and more economically than regular mail service. Subsidiaries of newspapers, magazines, and book publishers, and cable TV systems, telephone companies, banks, and retailers are using or promoting alternative ways of delivering data. General Telephone and Electronics (GTE), for example, offers Telenet and Telemail services that send letters and other messages electronically. The 1984 Olympic Games Organizing Committee recently announced that they will use Western Electric equipment for electronic mail to expedite transmission of results and messages to news media and Olympic support staff.

The use of the computer to send messages from one terminal to another is also growing.

As mail prices rise, technological advances are causing the cost of delivering a piece of electronic mail to decrease. According to Paris Burstyn, editor of "The Report on Electronic Mail" published by the Yankee Group in Boston, the basic cost of delivering a piece of electronic mail (from terminal to terminal via telephone lines) is now about 50 cents. That cost will fall to 25 cents by 1985.

Even though the cost involved in the transmission of some forms of electronic mail from terminal to terminal is greater than that of regular mail, electronic mail does have its advantages. Besides eliminating paper, delivery time involves seconds instead of days.

Electronic Computer-Originated Mail

As a response to a growing number of businesses switching to alternative mailing services, the Postal Service in January, 1982, began a new electronic mail service that businesses could use to have computerized bills and messages delivered with regular mail. The service is called Electronic Computer-Originated Mail (E-COM) and allows large-volume mailers to bypass traditional mail-handling methods in which a letter is sorted by various postal clerks before being delivered.

A company's computer will send a message via a communications carrier such as a telephone line (five telecommunications carriers have signed agreements to provide the link between the companys' computers and the Postal Service) to one of twenty-five post offices around the country that have been specially equipped to handle the messages. At the post office the message is printed on paper and inserted into a special E-COM envelope and delivered along with regular mail. Delivery time is a maximum of two days.

Businesses wishing to use E-COM must pay $50 a year plus 26 cents for the first page and 5 cents for the second page of a message. The common carrier must be paid separately. A minimum of 200 messages at a time must be sent within an area served by one of the twenty-five post offices.

Original projections of a first-year volume of 20 million pieces have been hampered by Justice and Commerce Department challenges, creating a wait and see attitude by many potential users of the system. The first three months of 1982 saw only 82,000 pieces of mail delivered through E-COM, far short of original projections. Long-range projections place volume at 500 million pieces a year, still less than 1 percent of the total volume of mail handled in a year.

For direct marketers E-COM has several limitations not found with regular mail. For example, E-COM does not allow for a return envelope. The Postal Service is, however, considering the addition of a return envelope as a mailing option.

Creative possibilities in mailer design are also limited. The envelopes are a uniform blue and white, and the messages are printed in a basic letter format with limited graphics.

THE FUTURE

What does the future hold for Teletext, Viewdata, and other interactive systems? The field is still in its infancy, with many companies going off in many different directions, experimenting with different hardware, software, and marketing techniques. At this stage in the development of the new technologies, most companies are not yet thinking in terms of profitability, but more in terms of trying to learn, trying to see how people respond to various product offerings and marketing techniques, and trying to determine how well they accept the new technologies.

Evolving interactive techniques utilizing increasingly sophisticated electronic technologies may very well be the next major growth area for direct marketers, but it may be some time yet before the potential of these technologies can be fully tapped. An article by Quelchand Takeuchi in the July/August 1981 *Harvard Business Review* entitled "Nonstore Marketing: Fast Track or Slow," summarized the potential of interactive in this way: "There is little reason to expect that consumers will soon take to (the new technologies) in large numbers, and they offer few if any usable techniques for making their selling tasks easier. The actual impact of the new technology will be minimal (before 1990)."

A more upbeat prediction in the March, 1982, edition of *DM News* was a quote from a study by International Resource Development, entitled "Television as the Home Communications Terminal." The study suggested that two-way television, including related products and services, will become a $9-billion industry by 1990.

Roadblocks to Growth

Before these new technologies can truly take hold, several significant roadblocks to growth need to be resolved. First of all, the technology, which is improving all the time, needs to be installed in enough homes to make interactive TV worthwhile. At the present time only a relatively small number of homes across the nation are wired for interactive TV, and it is uncertain how rapidly interactive growth will take place. One of the problems being encountered is the proliferation of various kinds of hardware and software, much of which is incompatible with other systems. That is, one system could not be used to access data from another system. In 1980, CBS recommended a national standard for teletext systems in an attempt to solve one of the problem areas of incompatibility, and to encourage uniform growth of interactive technology. Just recently, ABC and NBC accepted this recommended standard. It is hoped that the FCC will now adopt these standards.

Another apparently unresolved question is who should and should not be allowed to be information providers to the interactive data bases. The *Wall Street Journal* (7/19/82) reported that the American Newspaper Publishers Association was trying to get legislation to block AT&T from being able to use its telephone lines to transmit AT&T-prepared information, theoretically to protect the flow of information from being controlled by a monopoly. The ANPA saw AT&T as a direct threat to the future of newspaper publishing because the possibility exists that in the next decade we may be reading our news on computer terminals instead of on paper.

The proposed legislation by the ANPA was made moot by an agreement between AT&T and the Justice Department to a change in their antitrust settlement (*Wall Street Journal* 8/12/82). U.S. District Judge Harold H. Greene, who has final approval on the settlement, said he would not approve it until several conditions were met. One of those conditions was that AT&T agree not to use its own facilities to create an electronic information service for at least seven years. Judge Greene stated that if AT&T develops its own service, it "could use its control over the phone network to give priority to traffic from its own publishing operations over that of its competitors."

Another roadblock to growth is potential consumer resistance to the use of the computer to store and manipulate the information collected from interactive systems. With each purchase of a product, or with each response to an electronic opinion poll, or with each program that is watched, the computer is steadily building psychographic profiles of individual viewers, profiles that could conceivably be used in harmful or embarrassing ways. At the same time, the information gained is valuable, not only to the marketer, but also to the consumer. Marketers will be able to better target their sales messages to those consumers who are more apt to be interested in them. The marketer reduces the cost per product, and the consumer's time is not wasted by irrelevant advertising.

Ethical guidelines need to be firmly in place to ensure that the information gathered by computer and other means is used in a manner that is legally and morally correct. In addition, the industry needs to help consumers understand the kind of information that is being collected and how it will be used.

Your Involvement in the New Technologies

Can you afford to ignore the new technologies? Should you wait until the field is more developed before stepping in? The companies that are involved right now are learning and benefiting from getting their foot in the door at the beginning. Although profits now are low or nonexistent, those companies should be ahead of the game when competitors try to enter the field. Most companies, however, appear to be content to sit back and observe the development of interactive systems. One thing that is certain, though, is that you or your company should not dismiss the new technologies out of hand, and at the very least should keep your finger on the pulse of the industry. The potential exists for this sleeping giant to come to life sometime within this decade. The question is how soon it will happen and how big the industry will become.

Ogilvy and Mather, a respected worldwide direct response agency, cautions against ignoring the interactive arena even if you don't feel that it has application to your needs or your product or service. They believe that a fundamental change is underway in how people use their television, a change from passive acceptance to active participation. A younger generation is coming of age that has grown up with electronic games and computers. They are used to the push-button world of interactive technology. This new generation may virtually demand interactive features in their homes. Those advertisers and marketers who fail to take into consideration this new generation and their demographic and psychographic characteristics when creating commercial messages and direct-marketing promotions may find themselves unable to compete with those who have.

Capital investment into these new fields can be substantial and risky. The British, for example, have already invested more than $30 million in their Prestel system and anticipate an eventual investment of about $100 million. The installation of 30 million terminals in French households will also require many millions of dollars. Teletext and Viewdata systems might never have gotten off the ground as rapidly as they did, had not the British and French governments subsidized them. Now that these systems are up and running, and investors have had an opportunity to see their potential, investment will be perceived to be less of a risk than before.

But the technology is still evolving. There is the danger that millions of dollars may be invested into systems that may be out-of-date by the time they are completed, and many investors are taking a wait and see attitude for just this very reason. The world of electronic communication is extremely dynamic; new developments in this field may completely change the way we send and receive information.

Finally, the jury is still out on how the public will accept the new technologies. Testing to date has been either weak, inconclusive, or disappointing. Perhaps the only certainty in the experimental process is that the public is not yet used to interactive technology, since so few homes are wired for the service. The "catch 22" here is that investors and marketers are reluctant to commit significant resources until the public can show its approval or disapproval.

In the meantime, cable systems are expanding rapidly and EDM activity is increasing. Consumers are gradually learning that direct response is the way to complete a transaction quickly and conveniently, thereby making the transition from current direct response techniques to the interactive technologies of the future that much smoother.

Summary of Important Points

Viewdata is a *two-way* interactive system with a centrally located data base. Teletext is a *one-way* broadcast system with a centrally located, constantly transmitting data base.

Most Viewdata and Teletext systems are not sophisticated enough to transmit animation or coordinated sound. This limits the ways a marketer can present a product or service to the consumer.

Videodiscs and VCRs have potential for EDM, but direct marketers face problems of high cost, system incompatibility, and a lack of consumer acceptance.

Microcomputers can access any number of data bases, but as of yet they are limited in number because of high consumer cost; in addition, they are mostly "at home" self-contained systems not connected to a centralized data source.

Electronic mail is slowly gaining in popularity but has limited creative possibilities. Long-range projections place volumes at no more than 1 to 2 percent of total mail delivered.

Most experiments with the new technologies have not yet proved profitable, but there is tremendous potential. It is important that marketers, even if not currently anticipating involvement, continue to monitor their progress.

10

THE PRODUCT

Which products and services are best suited for promotion using EDM? That is a difficult question to answer; there are a number of factors that can determine the success or failure of the introduction of any product or service using EDM. For example, a product may be perfect for EDM, but a poorly conceived and developed promotion may eliminate any chance for success. A product may find new life under a different marketer using a different promotional approach. Perhaps the wrong electronic media were chosen, or the price was too high, or the promotion was geared toward the wrong target market. For these reasons and others that we will explore, the determination of what is a good product or service to promote using EDM is a difficult one. In the final analysis the only way to know the potential of your product and promotion in the electronic media is to test.

Historically, the greatest proportion of EDM promotions was done by a few firms offering a very narrow line of products. By the mid-1970s record, tape, book, and magazine sales accounted for nearly 70 percent of total expenditures for EDM promotions. Today we are seeing an increasing number and variety of products sold through EDM, but the same relatively narrow line of products still accounts for a significant portion of EDM expenditures.

Magazine publishers, for example, find that it is still possible to acquire subscriptions at a satisfactory cost per sale. *Time, Newsweek,* and *Sports Illustrated,* among many others, spend a major portion of their total advertising dollars for EDM promotions. These publishers are becoming increasingly sophisticated in their use of EDM, using direct-lead, direct-sale, and support EDM where it is most effective. These publishers, as well as other large EDM users, are also able to keep their costs for radio and television time at a minimum. This is because they are able to negotiate for larger blocks of less expensive time than the smaller direct marketer.

Magazine, book, and newspaper publishers are also heavy users of the telephone to generate subscription sales. Most publishers have found that it is cost effective to contact readers whose subscriptions have expired or are about to expire. The two basic approaches most publishers use to renew subscriptions are to (1) send a direct-mail piece reminding the customer of an impending subscription expiration (the mail piece would include the usual response option of a coupon or toll-free number) and follow this up with a direct telephone contact from the publisher, or, (2) contact the consumer one or more times by telephone only. It is not uncommon for a reluctant subscriber to receive three or more direct-mail pieces and two or more telephone contacts from the publisher. If all this seems expensive for the publisher, it is. But it has been found that the cost is less for the renewal effort than the cost of acquiring new subscribers.

AN EXAMINATION OF EDM PRODUCT AND SERVICE CRITERIA

Mass Appeal or Narrow Appeal?

Books, magazines, records, and many gadgets have been and will probably continue to be marketed successfully using EDM. The public has become accustomed to seeing these products marketed in this way and are increasingly accepting EDM as the way in which these products are to be purchased. But with acceptance of these products comes public awareness and acceptance of EDM in general. The public is beginning to understand that not only is it easy to pick up the phone to order a book or magazine; it is just as easy to purchase any number of products and services the same way. This increasing awareness should make it easier in the future to offer products that have never been offered through EDM. Telephone direct marketers, for example, are beginning to find that it is possible to sell anything from storm windows to motivation courses to rug shampoo simply by calling the prospect and determining his or her needs.

A wide variety of services are also being offered using EDM techniques, and the opportunity exists for virtually any service to be offered using EDM.

Charitable organizations, consulting firms (engineering, business, management, investment), volunteer organizations, travel agencies, the armed services, churches, mechanics, health clubs, telecommunications companies (television, radio, telephone), transportation services (trucking, airlines, rail), cleaning services, and even professional services such as lawyers, dentists, and CPAs, are finding success with EDM promotions.

Products that have had the most success on television and radio were those that had the characteristic of mass appeal. That is, the majority of viewers reached by the media were possible consumers of the product being advertised. This mass appeal factor, combined with low-priced commercial time, allowed direct marketers to profit with EDM. Products with mass appeal continue to make up the greatest proportion of EDM promotions.

Marketers are now beginning to offer products on radio and television that are directed toward a very narrow audience, a promotion technique that was thought to be unprofitable by direct marketers until very recently. A product with narrow appeal meant targeting audiences using high-priced commercial time, necessitating greater revenues to offset higher overhead costs. Results so far have been very promising. Exxon, for example, found that it was profitable to use a two-step television EDM process to sell their QWIP office product (a relatively expensive product with a limited target market).

As long as results can be monitored using the measurement tools inherent in EDM, the feasibility of marketing a product with narrow or mass appeal is simply a question of insuring that an acceptable number of responses occurs for each EDM promotion.

Quality

Because of the types of products historically sold through EDM, consumers have developed a general perception that the products they buy through EDM will not necessarily be of the highest quality. Years of hearing and seeing fast-talking salesmen pitching gadgets on late night programs have turned off the interest of many potential consumers. Consumers are not as naive as many marketers tend to treat them. Consumers are increasingly aware of their rights and can be very vocal when it comes to complaining about shoddy marketing practices and products. Anything you do to destroy consumer confidence in your business will come back to haunt you and your business. Not only must your marketing operations be clean in terms of ethics, but the products you offer should be of acceptable quality. There are several reasons for this.

First of all, EDM is a highly visible marketing technique, especially in the area of television and radio. Consumers are smart enough to tell if you are offering them a product they can count on. Even if you can fool them into ordering a poor product, returns from dissatisfied customers can be devastating. It is not unheard of to have returns as high as 25 to 30 percent. Not only will you find that you have created an unprofitable promotion, but you will also find it extremely difficult to continue to do business with any radio or television stations. Bad products are the station's problem, too, and one they would just as soon not deal with. Stations are very sensitive to the complaints of consumers because those complaints are one of the factors that are used to determine whether or not the station can renew its license to operate.

If you are in competition with other marketers trying to buy time, station managers will more than likely choose those marketers that they have had the least trouble with. On the other hand, if you have achieved a good reputation with your customers and with the stations you have dealt with, your next product promotion will be met with more acceptance from the consumer, and you will find it much easier to deal with the stations.

Your ability to build a solid customer base and your ability to continue to derive revenues from that base hinges on your products and the type of service you have provided to them. If they like your products, they will be more inclined to continue to do business with you. And even if you do not intend to sell to your past customers, your list of past customers can be valuable to others.

Copying Success

Should you try to sell the same product that others are selling, or should you attempt to market a product that is unique to EDM? Marketers have for years been marketing similar products with little deviation, but there is reason to believe that the EDM marketplace is wide open to a much wider variety of product offerings. As long as the sales message can be presented, the promotion properly monitored, and an adequate delivery system set up, there is no reason that anything that can be purchased through a retail outlet cannot just as easily be purchased using one of the channels of EDM.

Some marketers advocate the practice of studying products that are doing well and obtaining those or similar products for promotion. These marketers claim that by copying products in this way, much of the risk is taken out of their own promotion. The pioneer of a product has less of an advantage because he or she will be making mistakes along the way and must bear much of the testing cost to determine its viability. By waiting until only the survivor products are left, you then can pick from the most successful for your own.

Trying to copy others' successes may not be as easy as it sounds. First of all, it is difficult to accurately calculate the success rate of any EDM promotion. Since the marketer is not about to tell you how successful a promotion is, about the only way to tell if it is successful is to observe its rate of appearance in the media. If the promotion is successful, generally the marketer will step up the number of times the advertisement is shown. But with EDM, the length of time an ad will run is generally a short-lived phenomenon. After a few weeks, most EDM ads, even the most successful, will have begun to lose their pull and will be quickly taken off the air. If you were to copy the product, you would more than likely not be as successful as the original marketer because the original marketer would have saturated the market for the product.

You will probably be much more successful finding a product with which you are comfortable and testing it yourself. The initial risk may be a bit greater, but the potential for higher returns will more than offset that risk.

If you have a product that you would like to market but are worried that it may be copied as soon as it is advertised, then EDM is probably the best marketing technique to use to prevent that from happening. EDM lets you get into the marketplace quickly, and, if your product is successful, will allow you to saturate that marketplace before your competition can react.

Getting Your Invention into the Marketplace

Perhaps you have invented a product and would like to either market it yourself or find a company to market it for you.

As you may have already discovered, marketing an invention can be a difficult and frustrating process. There are thousands of inventors who have spent years trying to convince others of the sales potential of their products.

EDM can provide the spark that gets your product into the marketplace; without expending a lot of capital, you can get an indication of your product's sales potential.

If you can show a company sales projections based on proven performance, your chances of getting that company to take on your product are greatly enhanced. And you will also be in a superior negotiating position when royalties are discussed.

Product Relationship

The building of a cohesive customer base is an important consideration of the marketer who wishes to diversify his or her business later to take advantage of the potential value of those customers. As you evaluate products you might promote using EDM, it may be to your advantage to select products that are similar to each other or are members of the same product line. By selecting and promoting similar products, you will be obtaining customers who, if they like your products, may be persuaded to purchase the same or similar products in the future. If you have developed a product line related to products that have been purchased by your EDM customers, you can then promote your product line to those customers using other forms of direct marketing such as catalogs or direct mail.

This procedure of building a solid customer base is basic to the direct-marketing business. Your customers are your most valuable asset, an asset that can be used again and again, even while you continue to promote your products using EDM. Most major direct marketing catalog and mail-order businesses got their start by advertising their products one at a time, mostly in the print media—magazines and newspapers. More and more of these large direct marketers are moving into the electronic media instead of, or in addition to, the print media to expand their customer base.

Determining Price

Price is one of the most important variables a consumer considers when deciding to purchase. If the price is too high (that is, considered to be too high by the consumer, the price may be the minimum at which you can sell to make a reasonable profit), you will have dismal sales even though your product may be the very best.

Or your price may be too low and you may be unable to generate a sufficient volume of orders per promotion to break even.

Of course, the eventual price you charge for your product must take into consideration *all* of your costs—product cost, overhead, advertising, and so on—and still include enough of a margin to provide an acceptable profit to you. You will be able to determine, with a certain volume of orders per promotion, a price below which all of your cost and profit criteria cannot be met.

Price has an influence in determining the type of media you will use, whether or not you will be using a one-step (direct sale), or two-step (direct lead) process, and, if you've chosen radio or TV, will also have an influence on commercial length.

There are no hard and fast rules regarding prices in the electronic media, but some generalizations can be made. The average price range of products successfully sold using *direct sale* EDM on radio and television is about $7 to $20. Products offered for less than and considerably more than these prices are rare and do not usually last. The $7 to $20 range seems to be psychologically acceptable as not being too much money to risk when purchasing on impulse. With prices any higher than this, the consumer cannot be motivated to act within the 30- to 120-second timeframe of the average direct sales spot.

In general, the higher priced the product is, the greater the amount of convincing that will be required to justify the price of the product. The best way to convince the consumer of the value of a product is to let the media do the talking. The media that can most adequately and efficiently portray this value will produce the greatest response to your promotion. For example, the value of a product may be obvious as soon as the consumer sees it in operation. Marketers have for years taken advantage of television EDM to illustrate value. An example of an EDM commercial that illustrates value is the now-famous late night stainless steel bowl commercial where an actor stands on his head with his full weight on the bowl. Not only are the toughness and durability of the product amply proven, but at the end of the commercial, all of the bowls and accessories are spread across the screen, with the announcer emphasizing that "you can get *all* this for the low price of only $————." The esthetics of the ad left a bit to be desired, of course, but it was extremely successful, in major part because the consumer was able to see the worth of the product. Another medium would have been less successful. For example, it would have been difficult to describe the product over the telephone or the radio. The consumer would not have been able to value the product accurately without seeing it first.

High Price: Direct Sale or Direct Lead?

The higher the product's price, the more time that will normally be required to present it. Most consumers will balk at making an impulse purchase above a certain price. That price will vary depending on the type of product being offered. If the product is an obvious bargain compared with others in its category, then the price will not be an inhibiting factor in the consumer's decision to purchase. If the question of quality and "hidden catches," can be overcome in the allocated time, then the higher-priced item offered at a bargain can be sold successfully through direct sale EDM.

If all price objections cannot be overcome in the initial EDM presentation (direct sale), and if time is a factor, especially if you are using radio or television, then a direct lead format will probably be necessary.

One of the highest priced products ever offered for direct sale on television was a $1250 limited edition artist's print. The EDM commercial was 120 seconds in length, with twenty seconds devoted to ordering information. Results of the promotion were not disclosed.

Another recent television EDM promotion offered a $200 me-

142

dallion in a direct sales format. The medallion was struck with the name of the consumer's college alma mater. The commercial was sixty seconds long; thirty seconds of that time was used to display the address and telephone number, leaving only thirty seconds for the sales presentation.

The commercial was not successful. Sixty seconds was not enough time to justify the $200 purchase price. Today's consumer is not yet used to making a $200 impulse purchase based on such limited information. The only way to provide the consumer with more information in a television EDM environment is either to increase the length of the commercial presentation, or to convert the presentation into a two-step process, perhaps offering to send a brochure containing additional information.

Perhaps another type of direct-response promotion for the medallion would have been more effective. For example, a mailing list could have been obtained of all alumni of various institutions. A package of information about the medallion could have been mailed to the alumni, with follow-up telephone calls used as support to the mailings.

Telephone selling offers you the opportunity to sell higher-priced products to consumers or other businesses in a one-step process. Because the telephone allows your salespeople to spend more time with your customers than does radio or television EDM, and because a two-way interaction is achieved where objections can be met and overcome and where your salespeople can establish themselves as people, it is not unheard of to complete transactions of several thousand dollars with a single phone call.

Of course, all the electronic media have been used to sell almost any type of product or service at almost any price. Those products or services that cannot be sold in a one-step process almost certainly lend themselves to the two-step selling process. The two-step process is how almost all higher-priced products are sold using EDM. As when the telephone is used, the direct lead process allows the marketer to spend more time with the customer, time that is efficiently spent with a customer who already has expressed an interest in your product.

The Trend Toward Direct-Sale EDM

Because the two-step process implies that there is some time between the initial and follow-up contact, there is the possibility, especially if the product is an impulse item, that the customer will have lost interest and will not purchase. The more products that can be sold through direct sale, then, the better. With the one-step process the customer is purchasing immediately, while the impulse to buy is still strong. What then will contribute to the marketer's being able to offer higher-priced products for direct sale using television or radio EDM?

First of all, a change in consumer behavior is needed. The consumer must be convinced that it is perfectly natural to pick up the telephone in response to an ad and place an order for merchandise at aggregate prices above those historically offered in a direct sales mode. The best way to convince the consumer to do this is to spend more time with him or her, in many cases more time than is possible in a regular EDM promotion. Marketers are beginning to experiment on cable TV channels, not only with longer commercials, but also with actual programs designed to display several products one after the other in a catalog-type format. These programs are proving to be successful in moving merchandise not normally effectively sold using direct sale EDM on television.

Low-Priced Products

At the other end of the pricing spectrum is the price below which it ceases to be profitable to sell. It appears that $7 is the historical bottom of EDM product prices. The main reason that a price below about $7 is not feasible is that usually a commercial spot is not able to generate enough order volume to make the promotion worthwhile. There are of course exceptions to this rule. Products have been successfully sold for as low as $2 and $3.

You may be less concerned about turning a profit with your promotion than you are about developing a list of customers that can eventually generate more sales through direct mail or personal selling. In that case you would keep the price of your product at a minimum to attract names. About the only approach that has proved profitable in selling lower-priced products using EDM is to offer those products in groups of two or three or more. This pricing procedure effectively increases your revenue per order. One television EDM promotion a few years ago offered a set of sanding tools that, if sold individually, would have generated insufficient income to make the promotion profitable. Another marketer used telephone direct selling to market the sale and development of fim. The film was sold in packages of several rolls each.

FINDING NEW PRODUCTS

Even if you have a product that is ideal for the electronic media, you may soon need to be searching for new products. Not only are most marketers never able to build a business on just one product, but, because of EDM's ability to saturate the target market, especially the consumer market, in a relatively short time, even a wildly successful promotion using EDM can be short-lived. You must therefore be prepared to come on-line with new products as soon as your currently promoted product loses its pulling power.

Where should you start your search? You should probably examine your own interests and products that relate to those interests. What is your background? What are your hobbies? Are you sports-minded? Do you like to garden?

If you are presently running a retail business, what type of products are you selling? What products do you know best? There may be a natural product here, but you must be cautious in your choice. The choice of a product from an area of your interest may prejudice you into selecting a product that may have a low probability for success.

Do you own a small business? Do you sell a product that might lend itself to EDM? We describe in Chapter Two how a clothing store used EDM and catalogs to sell its clothing line. Harry and David, now Harry and David, Inc., turned their local fruit store into a nationwide operation by selling their fruit through direct marketing channels.

Are you an expert on something? Write a book or design a course. Several authors have successfully self-promoted their works using television and radio EDM.

Are you a retailer working for a large department store? Most of the major department stores now generate a significant portion of their revenue through catalog sales, and the telephone is a primary response tool. Some department stores are now beginning to experiment with television EDM to promote the sale of individual items, and to obtain new customers to whom they can mail their catalogs. Perhaps your retailer could make use of EDM in some way.

There may be a product that appeals to you in a current promotion in one of the electronic media.

Attend home-improvement shows, auto shows, electronics fairs, inventors' fairs, trade fairs, and craft fairs. One marketer used television EDM to successfully market hand puppets found at a craft fair.

Look in specialty stores or department stores. Perhaps you know of a product that is not selling well in a retail store because it requires the explanation or demonstration that EDM can provide. But be careful. With a product that can be found in local retail stores, unless you have something unique to offer, such as a lower price or better quality, you are essentially providing free advertising to local retailers. If you do find a product in a retail outlet that you feel has potential, perhaps you can convince the distributor or manufacturer that you can move the product through the EDM channel.

There may be success in a previous EDM failure. Perhaps the product could have been promoted differently, or perhaps the product is now coming into vogue. You may even be able to revitalize an older successful EDM promotion.

Examine import catalogs from other countries. Travel to Europe or other countries. Become aware of trends there. Contact foreign consulates in our country. They will be happy to assist you in your search for new products and can provide you with information, including regulations and names and addresses of firms to contact.

Examine successful promotions in other direct marketing media. Check old and new mail-order ads for ideas. Many directly marketed items in other media are transferable to the electronic media.

Run classified ads stating that you are looking for new products. Conversely, there may be other classified ads describing products for which others are trying to find distributors.

Examine the economy. How about products to help cope with inflation or save energy?

Finding the Manufacturer

Once you have found a product that you think might have potential, there are several ways to track down the manufacturer or distributor. If the product is in a retail store, simply ask the retailer for the name of the distributor, or note the address on the packaging. Your local library is a good source of product information, especially if you have an idea of the general type of product you would like to promote. Most libraries contain a *Thomas Register* or a *MacRae's Blue Book*, which list manufacturers by product category. Larger libraries will contain other directories, such as the *Gift and Decorative Accessories Directory*, the *Premium Suppliers' Directory*, or the *Encyclopedia of Trade Associations*.

Another good source of information is the Manhattan classified telephone directory. It contains almost every conceivable type of product manufacturer.

Practical Considerations

Once you think you have found your product or have narrowed your choices down to a few specific products, you might want to try to answer the following questions to see if those products are appropriate for the electronic media.

How does your product work? Does it work as well as the manufacturer or inventor says it does? Try it yourself. Give it to friends to try.

Is assembly required? Are the instructions clear? Have someone not familiar with the product try to assemble it. You may need to write your own instructions.

Is it dangerous? If someone gets hurt, who is responsible? Will you need liability insurance?

Can it be easily duplicated? Will it be easy for a competitor to jump in if you are successful?

Is it seasonal? Timing may be important. Are you considering an item that may only sell at one time during the year? Is it faddish? Will you potentially be stuck with a huge inventory if the fad dies? Could you use the excess inventory as a discounted loss leader or as a give-away with another product?

Do you have a regional item? Will it sell elsewhere if you roll out your promotion? Remember to first test your product in several diverse markets.

Does the product fit your standard for quality? Does it fit your company image? Does the product meld with the rest of your product line?

Does the product meet your cost criteria? Are fixed costs and margins reasonable?

Does the product have a chance of becoming obsolete? The Bowmar Brain, for example, was the first mass-produced electronic hand-held calculator. It was successfully sold through direct mail and space ads using the "800" number for response, but was soon competing against lower-priced, smaller, more versatile calculators. The company that manufactured the Bowmar soon succumbed to the competition. The direct marketer who promoted the Bowmar, however, saw the superior competition on the horizon. He was able to get out with a profit and was not stuck with a huge inventory of unsellable merchandise.

Is the product bulky? Are its dimensions awkward? Is it fragile?

How will you distribute the product to your customers? Mail? UPS? Personal delivery? Freight?

Can you obtain standard mailing packaging, or will it need to be custom made? Try mailing the package to yourself or a friend across the country. Did the product survive?

Negotiating for Products

Your ability to find a supplier and successfully negotiate for the rights to distribute a product is a function of your negotiating experience, your reputation, your personality, your proven selling performance, and the resources you are willing to commit to that product.

The supplier is just as eager as you are to see the product move, and if you can convince him or her that you will be able to sell a significant number of them, there should be no problem in working out some kind of an acceptable agreement.

When negotiating with a manufacturer or wholesaler for the

right to distribute a product, there are several key points that you should either try to address while negotiating or include in your final agreement.

1. Can you get the exclusive rights to the product? If not, can you get the exclusive mail-order rights? If you are successful, you do not want a dozen other competitors acquiring the same product from the same supplier. With exclusive distribution rights, you will have several options if your promotion proves successful. You may want to eventually market your product through alternative channels such as retail outlets. Several marketers have done just that. K-Tel Corporation, for example, now sells many of its products through retail outlets.

Gaining exclusive rights also means that you will not be competing with the same product in retail stores.

Some suppliers may be reluctant to give you distribution rights to a product beyond a specific area—three or four states, for example. This type of agreement will seriously hamper your ability to roll out an EDM promotion. You may saturate your area within a few weeks. Also, the electronic media broadcast beyond state boundaries, and you may impinge on another's territory without realizing it.

2. How much of the product does the supplier have on hand? How quickly can he or she provide additional products to you if your promotion takes off? Remember, response to an EDM promotion can be extremely volatile. You may have a need for thousands of additional products within virtually a moment's notice. It is vitally important that you do not have huge backorders. First of all, by law you are required to deliver your product to your customer within thirty days of the order. Secondly, your customers are valuable. You need to keep them satisfied.

How will the product be supplied to you? Will it be in bulk, necessitating additional labor on your part for repackaging or for mailing? Or, will the supplier provide your product mail-ready? If it is mail-ready, is the package acceptable to you? Would you need to add anything to it? Will the packaging meet your strength requirements for mailing?

Who will store the products? If you are a small company, you will have limited space for storage.

If your supplier will store your products for you, will he or she also drop-ship them? That is, if you provide the supplier with the names and addresses of those who ordered the products from your promotion, will he or she apply the addresses to the packages and mail them? There are many suppliers who drop-ship for their customers. You should try ordering several samples and have them delivered to various addresses around the country. Also, be sure to get a guarantee from the supplier that he or she will not use the names you are providing as a source for his or her own mailing list. Those names are very valuable and are worth keeping for your exclusive use.

3. How many products should you initially order? This is a difficult question to answer. You may have some idea as to the relative amount you will need based on previous experience selling a similar product. Or you may have tested your product and developed a projected need for your roll-out. It is probably safe to assume that you will require at least enough to reach your break-even point. A successful EDM promotion can quickly drain your inventory, however. You should have your supplier prepared to provide you with amounts above your break-even point on a moment's notice.

Your supplier may require you to order a minimum amount. Make sure this amount is not too far in excess of your break-even point, or you may be stuck with a warehouse full of products.

You may want to work out an agreement that stipulates that you will purchase a certain amount based upon whether or not your test promotion is successful. Or, for example, you might guarantee a minimum purchase of x amount per quarter or twelve-month period. If any amount below that is ordered, the rights to the product revert back to the supplier. The main idea is not to commit to too much quantity of a product but to ensure availability should the need arise.

4. How much can you afford to pay for your product? Your cost analysis will provide you with an acceptable price. It is important that you do not pay more per product than you had originally calculated to be acceptable. (Most EDM products have a mark-up of three to five times cost.) A price above your original calculations will significantly affect the final retail price and may make it unacceptable to consumers.

5. What terms do you need from your suppliers? Determine the terms before negotiating. If you cannot get the terms you think you need, try another supplier or another product. Let the numbers you have developed speak for you, and don't be tempted to commit yourself to an agreement that differs from your analysis. Remember, there are literally thousands of products that can be sold successfully through EDM. It will be worth your while to select those that can be obtained on terms acceptable to you.

Summary of Important Points

Although products with mass appeal continue to make up a large portion of EDM promotions, narrow-appeal products and services are also being successfully marketed. The main criterion to observe

in marketing any product or service is to test to insure that response satisfies cost and margin requirements.

Merchandise should be of highest quality. Always offer a guarantee. Keep your customers and the stations with which you work happy.

It is not advisable to copy others' successes. On the other hand, if you don't want to be copied or are concerned about others copying your idea, EDM will let you saturate the marketplace before others can get started.

Build a cohesive customer base by offering products along similar lines.

Price is dependent on product cost, customer perception of value, and the volume of orders per sales contact.

Price will influence your choice of direct sale or direct lead formats. A high-priced item or service always requires sufficient selling time to justify its cost.

The search for new products requires an assessment of your personal interests, your current line of business, your experience, and a concentrated examination of the needs of the marketplace.

Negotiation for rights to a product should include mail-order rights and an assurance that enough quantity of the product will be available in volatile sales situations.

APPENDIX

EDM GUIDELINES

Although there are a multitude of regulations that apply to all direct-marketing, advertising, and basic business operations, there are no federal regulations that specifically address broadcast EDM. Part of this lack of restrictive legislation is a reflection of the Direct Mail/Marketing Association philosophy that self-regulation is preferable to governmental regulation. Self-regulation affords a flexibility that lets marketers adjust to social, economic, or technological changes much easier than legislation that, once imposed, becomes difficult to modify.

The DMMA suggests that most potential broadcast EDM problems can be eliminated by submitting your commercial for approval under the code of the National Association of Broadcasters. Once approved, most legal and consumer problems will have been discovered and rectified.

Most of the problems associated with television and radio EDM promotions are a result of either misrepresentation or nondelivery of merchandise after the commercial has aired. As an example, there have been marketers who have put together EDM promotions and tested them for response without first having secured or even manufactured the promoted product. If response appeared to be poor, the promotion was cancelled and the money returned. If response was favorable, products were obtained or manufactured to meet the demand. Unfortunately, among other problems, delivery times became intolerable and consumers rightly complained. Today most broadcast stations request that a supply of the merchandise be maintained at the station. Consumer complaints of nondelivery made to the station can be satisfied immediately.

Most stations will request that you state merchandise delivery times in your offer. According to the FTC, you must ship your merchandise within thirty days of the receipt of an order, but you should make every effort to provide the merchandise to your customers as soon as possible. Many marketers send a confirmation postcard to the consumer as soon as the order is received. This helps to reduce customer complaints about nondelivery.

The DMMA suggests that, before starting any direct marketing business, you obtain copies of their "Guidelines for Acceptance of Direct Response Broadcast Advertising," "Guidelines for Acceptance of Direct Response Print Advertising," and "Personal Information Protection Guidelines." These can be obtained by writing to: DMMA; 6 East 43rd Street; New York, NY 10017.

You should also obtain copies of postal rules and regulations from your local post office, a copy of the code of the National Association of Broadcasters, and the FTC pamphlet that outlines types of unfair business methods and practices.

Make yourself aware of any state and local regulations that might apply to your marketing operation. These regulations are being constantly changed and updated, particularly in the area of telephone marketing. A summarized list of guidelines that specifically address telephone marketing is provided for you in Chapter Seven.

Staying within the appropriate legal and ethical parameters of direct marketing certainly makes good business sense. Stated another way, if you treat customers as you would like to be treated, how can you lose?

BIBLIOGRAPHY

"American Bell to Sell Sceptre Home Videotex Terminals." *AT&T Management Report*, July, 1983.

Arbitron Television. San Francisco: American Research Bureau, 1982.

Bernbach, William. "Be Sure Advertising Says Something With Substance." *Direct Marketing* (July 1977), pp. 22–28.

Bernhard, Henry. "Negative Attitudes Key to Exploring Direct Mail Myths." *Direct Marketing* (June 1978), p. 22.

Black, Norman. "Cable TV Industry Growing, But So Are Problems." *Journal American* (Bellevue, Wash.) April 15, 1982.

Booth, Alan. "Lower Cost Per Order Is Answer to Direct Mail Dilemma." *Mark II* (April 1977), pp. 16–17, 24.

Bury, Charles. *Telephone Techniques That Sell*. New York: Warner Books, 1980.

Caples, John. "How to Test T.V. Commercials Through Direct Response." *Direct Marketing* (September 1977), pp. 62–63, 83.

————. *Tested Advertising Methods*. 4th ed. Englewood Cliffs, N.J.: Prentice-Hall, 1978.

Cole, Tony. "Direct Marketing—More Ways Than One." *Marketing 'London'* (April 1976), pp. 70–71.

Cunningham-Reid, John. "Can Direct Sales Conquer T.V.?" *Marketing* (U.K.), Vol. 3, No. 32, November 19, 1980, pp. 35–37.

Direct Response Broadcast and New Electronic Media. New York: The Direct Mail Marketing Association, 1980.

"Electronic Mail Attracts Few Customers." *Journal American* (Bellevue, Wash.), April 23, 1982.

Fabian, Michael R. "Media Interrelationship-Maximizing Sales Impact." *Direct Marketing* (October 1976), pp. 26–36, 133.

Fact Book on Direct Response Marketing. 1982 ed. New York: The Direct Mail Marketing Association, Inc.

Gage, Theodore J. "Two-Way T.V. Screening Out the Bugs." *Advertising Age,* (January 18, 1982), pp. S–2, 6.

Galginaitis, Carol. "Catalogs Build Retailer's Reach Past City Limits." *Advertising Age* (January 18, 1982), pp. S-30–31.

Gildenhar, Jan. "After a Slow Start, Cable Gains Ground." *Seattle Times,* May 28, 1981.

Goldman, Jane. "Cable Markets the Best Buys: a New Vision for Shoppers." *Cable T.V. Magazine* (April, 1981), pp. 20–21, 32–33.

Gregory, Lon B. "Junk Calls—How Much a Problem." *Telephone Engineering and Management,* (June 1, 1979, vol. 83, n.11), pp. 99–103.

Hoge, Sr., Cecil C. *Mail Order Moonlighting.* Berkeley, Ca.: Ten Speed Press, 1976.

Kleppner, Otto. *Advertising Procedure.* Englewood Cliffs, N.J.: Prentice-Hall, 1979.

Levy, Sy, and Barbara Lewis. "T.V. Support Can Increase Response 50% or More." *Direct Marketing,* (September, 1977), p. 50–56.

Lieb, Jerome S. "Penetrating Television Market Using Direct Marketing Skills." *Direct Marketing,* (September, 1977), pp. 22–26.

Lionel, D. "Researcher Finds T.V. Hypos Stuffer Results." *Editor and Publisher,* (December 13, 1975).

Nash, Edward L.. *Direct Marketing: Strategy/Planning/Execution.* New York: McGraw-Hill Book Company, 1982.

Northup, Brent. "Video Newspapers? KIRO to Demonstrate New Teletext System." *Journal American,* (August 26, 1982).

"On the Horizon." *DM News,* (March 15, 1982), pp. 22–23.

Ostrow, J.W. "T.V. or Not T.V. That's Question Direct Marketers Must Answer." *Direct Marketing* (January, 1976), pp. 44–45, 53.

Porter, Sylvia. "Electronic Mail: Problems With Postal System Spurs Much New Development." *Seattle Times,* (July 20, 1981).

Quelch, John A., and Hirotaka Takeuchi. "Nonstore Marketing: Fast Track or Slow?" *Harvard Business Review* (July–August, 1981), pp. 75–84.

Roman, Murray. "Mail Plus Phone Makes Positive Option Offer Succeed." *Direct Marketing*, (April 1978), pp. 46–47.

"Ruling Protects Newspapers in Electronic Publishing." *Journal American* (Bellevue, Wash.), (December 8, 1982).

Sawyer, Robert A. "Direct Marketing: The Shape of Things to Come." *Advertising Age* (January 18, 1982), pp. S-1, S-48–50.

Simon, Julian L. *How to Start and Operate a Mail-Order Business.* 2nd ed. New York: McGraw-Hill Book Company, 1976.

Smith, George W. "When Opportunity Rings, Answer it with Analysis of Capabilities, Experience: Choosing the Right '800' InWATS Service." *Zip* (October, 1980), vol. 3, n. 8, pp. 34, 36.

Spot Television Rates and Data. Skokie, Ill.: Standard Rate and Data Service, Inc., 1982.

Standard Directory of Advertising Agencies. Skokie, Ill.: National Register Publishing Company, Inc., 1982.

Stone, Bob. "Direct Marketers Live Not By Mail Alone." *Advertising Age* (March 6, 1978), pp. 48, 55.

―――. "Direct Response Advertisers Have Little Concern for Nielson Ratings." *Advertising Age* (November 7, 1977), p. 64.

―――. *Successful Direct Marketing Methods.* Chicago: Crain Books, 1980.

Sugarman, Joseph. *Success Forces.* Chicago: Contemporary Books, 1980.

Telephone Marketing. New York: Direct Mail Marketing Association, 1981.

"Telephone Marketing Demanding Increased Attention." *Industrial Marketing* (August, 1977, vol. 62, n. 8), pp. 83, 86.

"Television as the Home Communications Terminal." *DM News* (March, 1982), pp. 22–23.

"This New 'Telly' Will Change Our Lives." *The Sunday Times* (London) (December 30, 1979).

T.V. Fact Book. Washington, D.C.: Television Digest, 1982.

West, Gary. "OUT or IN, Dialing Delivers Dollars." *Advertising Age* (January 18, 1982), pp. S–39, 41.

INDEX

NOW ... *Announcing these other fine books from Prentice-Hall—*

THE FUTURE OF VIDEOTEXT: Worldwide Prospects for Home/Office Electronic Information Services, by Efrem Sigel, et al. Will there soon be a videotext system in every home? This and other questions are explored in this important survey of the current status of electronic information services around the world. It evaluates the possibilities for mass use—and the causes and cures of the past pitfalls—of this simple yet ingenious technology, describing the latest developments in videotext and teletext and how they stack up next to our other popular media.

$9.95 paperback $22.95 hardcover

HOW TO BUILD A MULTI-MILLION DOLLAR MAIL-ORDER CATALOG BUSINESS BY SOMEONE WHO DID, by Lawson Traphagen Hill. In this book, the founder of a leading mail-order leather and shoe firm reveals the dynamics of launching and sustaining a mail-order business through the special medium of the catalog. Covering all the basics with an emphasis on getting good graphics, it shows both beginners and professionals what it takes to succeed.

$15.95 paperback $24.95 hardcover

To order these books, just complete the convenient order form below and mail to **Prentice-Hall, Inc., General Publishing Division, Attn. Addison Tredd, Englewood Cliffs, N.J. 07632**

Title	Author	Price*
_____	_____	_____
_____	_____	_____
_____	_____	_____

Subtotal _____

Sales Tax (where applicable) _____

Postage & Handling (75¢/book) _____

Total $ _____

Please send me the books listed above. Enclosed is my check ☐ Money order ☐ or, charge my VISA ☐ MasterCard ☐ Account # _____

Credit card expiration date _____

Name _____

Address _____

City _____ State _____ Zip _____

Prices subject to change without notice. Please allow 4 weeks for delivery.